VICARIOUS
A LIFE LIVED THROUGH FOOD

K.J. BRADFORD

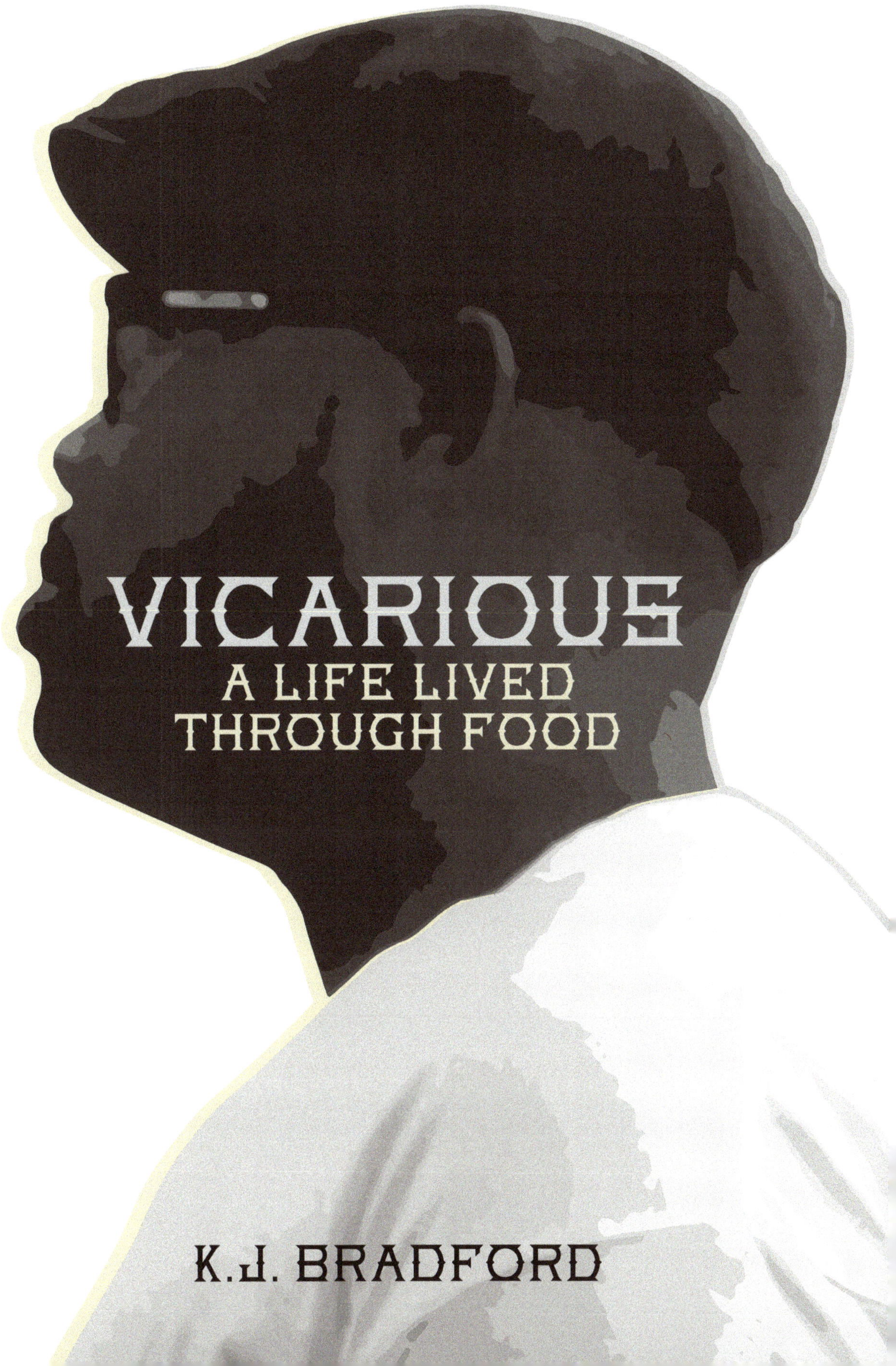

VICARIOUS

A LIFE LIVED THROUGH FOOD

K.J. BRADFORD

Back Porch Publishing, LLC
16081 Grace Lake Drive
Fairhope, AL 36532

ISBN 9798987269381

Cover Design & Layout: Virginia Mathers

Printed in the United States of America

Acknowledgments

This book is dedicated to the memory of my grandmother, Clara Goodman. She was more than a mentor in the kitchen; she instilled in me invaluable life lessons.

To my parents and my brother, thank you for your unwavering support and for always being in my corner.

To my friends, your encouragement made this journey so much smoother. Your support was the backbone during this process.

Live opulently, but eat VICARIOUSLY!

Table of Contents

Foreword

Vicariously. This is the best word to describe how I am living when I see the creations from Kellen Bradford's kitchen. After one bite of his dish, I know I must be living through someone else to taste something so delicious. Not only is his cooking a work of art, it is equally as delicious. Through his cookbook, many more people will be able to live vicariously through his delectable dishes in their own kitchens.

I have known Kellen for several years now. The first Kellen creation I experienced (I say experienced because it is an experience) was a lasagna dinner and tiramisu. Sounds simple? Wrong. To say he created the best lasagna and tiramisu I have ever eaten is no exaggeration. A mutual friend who studied in Rome, Italy, for five years testified that he had not eaten a better tiramisu during his entire tenure in Rome. Kellen did not leave any detail unfinished in his dinner that evening, and I know this cookbook has been compiled on the same level of diligence. Crafting delectable dishes is Kellen's passion, and he has chosen to share this passion with the world.

I am not the world's best cook and am nowhere close to the level of Kellen; however, this cookbook gives me the opportunity to appear to be as competent a chef as Kellen. Whether you are looking to feed your family or impress a date with your skills in the kitchen, this book will give you the ingredients for a successful and impressive meal. Your dining companion's taste buds are in for a real treat and their bellies for a satisfying meal. Learn to master the kitchen and the art of entertaining with food from Kellen's creations. Bring vicarious living to your loved ones through the new products of your kitchen. Become the culinary envy of your friends and enjoy the savory fruits of your labor.

Through this book, Kellen will take you along on a ride through the world's most delicious cuisines and desserts. You will learn to master his recipes and treat your guests and yourself to a rich meal from Kellen's vast knowledge of culinary arts. Prepare to impress any crowd with a dish from this book and enjoy every bite you take of your new creation. Page after page of this book is filled with recipes to expand your culinary horizons and enhance your palate. Your appreciation for spices and flavors, sweets and pastries will grow with each new recipe you try. Experience life in a new way through the food you prepare from Kellen's expert compilation of recipes.

Kellen is very passionate about sharing his meals with others and entertaining them through food. He is gracious to share the secrets of this passion with the world in this book. Join me in my quest to replicate this same passion by treating family and friends to Kellen's dishes. Let us all help our friends live vicariously through their food and expand their tastes and experiences. Through the use of Kellen's book, you can learn to bring joy and happiness to your loved ones through food and brighten a friend's day with a dessert.

Ladies and gentlemen, it is time to sharpen your knives and don your aprons. Get ready to live vicariously.

Living Vicariously,
Will Robbins

IN THE BEGINNING

PANTRY GUIDE

Your pantry, in essence, is your culinary canvas. When curated well, even simple meals can become a tantalizing dish.

A well-stocked pantry is a cornerstone of every kitchen, regardless of your culinary prowess. It's your safety net for those unexpected dinner plans or when a store run isn't feasible. Here's a list of pantry essentials to ensure you're always ready to whip up a meal.

1. Pasta

An ultimate savior for last-minute meals! Diversify your collection with:

Short Cuts: Macaroni, cavatelli, farfalle, and orzo.

Long Cuts: Fettuccine, spaghetti, tagliatelle, bucatini, and linguini.

Specialty: Lasagna noodles and shell pasta.

Frozen Varieties: Like tortellini for those quick dinners.

2. Grains

A fabulous way to enhance your meal options, grains are versatile in both savory and sweet dishes.

Rice: While the rice aisle can be overwhelming, a long grain variety works as an all-rounder. If space permits, also stock up on Arborio (short grain) and healthful brown rice.

Quick-cook Grains: Grits, polenta, bulgur wheat, and couscous are not just time savers but also pocket-friendly.

3. Legumes

High in protein and rich in nutrients, legumes are a must-have.

Beans: With countless varieties available, aim to have at least two bags of your preferred beans ready to go.

4. Canned Goods

While fresh is usually best, some canned goods are invaluable for convenience.

Tomatoes: Tomato paste, whole peeled tomatoes (especially San Marzano), and crushed tomatoes.

Beans: Canned chickpeas for a quick hummus, and pinto or black beans for soups or refried beans.

Milks: Coconut milk, condensed milk, and evaporated milk. A quality stock in a box is always handy too.

5. Spices

The flavor dynamo of your kitchen!

Essentials:

- Turmeric
- Chili Flakes
- Lavender
- Kosher or Sea Salt
- Coarse Black Pepper
- Chili Powder
- Nutmeg
- Cinnamon
- Ginger
- Curry Powder
- Cardamom (whole and ground)
- Fennel Seeds
- Coriander
- Star Anise

Storage Tip: Preserve the potency of spices by storing them in a cool, dark place and rotating regularly. Ideally, refresh your spice collection annually.

WINE GUIDE

Wine, a cherished libation, has graced our societies for ages. While I'm not a sommelier, I can certainly share some tips to enhance your wine-savvy persona. Let's begin by understanding the very essence of this beverage.

DIVING DEEP INTO THE WORLD OF WINE

Wines come in three main colors: red, white, and rosé, all usually with an alcohol content between 10 and 13 percent.

Red wines derive their deep hue from grape skins used during fermentation. When crafting red wine, the entire grape—skins, seeds, pulp, and stems—is crushed. This mixture, termed "must," heads straight to fermentation vats. The grape skins impart color, while the seeds and stems add, minerals, and other elements, all of which define red wine's taste and health-promoting properties.

White wines can be crafted from either white or black grapes. Though the crushing process is similar to that for red wine, when making white wine from black grapes, only the juice is fermented. Interestingly, the primary grape for Champagne is the black Pinot Noir. Lacking the skins, seeds, and stems during fermentation, white wines typically have a more delicate flavor. However, some white wines can rival the intensity of reds.

Rosé wines bridge the gap between reds and whites. Their pink hue can be achieved in a couple of ways. One approach is to crush the grapes as for red wine, but halt fermentation once the desired color is reached. Another technique combines both black and white grapes. The natural methods are preferable, and it's worth noting that rosés are best enjoyed young; aging rarely benefits them. You do not want a rosé with a stated vintage of more than three to four years back.

Now, with a grasp on wine varieties, let's discuss how to select, serve, and store your chosen bottle.

Selecting the Perfect Bottle

When buying wine, nothing beats the expertise of the source. Visiting a local winery or wine merchant can offer insights from someone familiar with the field. Always be candid about your wine experience, be it novice or connoisseur. Opt for a tasting session to discover your preferences. When in other venues, like restaurants or supermarkets, rely on your taste over popularity. Mail order is another viable option for wine purchase.

Serving Wine Like a Pro

Contrary to popular belief, most wines today are best enjoyed soon after opening. Yet, it's good practice to let them breathe for about an hour prior to serving.

Red wines reveal their full essence at room temperature and should never be chilled. For a swift serving of affordable reds, you can warm them slightly but spare your premium wines this treatment.

White wines, regardless of the season, are best served chilled. Dry or semi-dry variants need around 40 minutes in a fridge, while sparklers like Champagne require about an hour. Exquisitely sweet wines, like Sauternes, take longer, around an hour and 35 minutes. Dry fortified wines are good with a 40-minute chill, whereas ruby ports prefer ambient temperatures.

It's worth noting that quality wines often have sediment—decanting is recommended for mature reds.

Storing Your Bottles

For storage, seek a dry cabinet with consistent temperatures, away from strong odors that could compromise the wine's integrity through the cork.

Above all, wine enjoyment is subjective. Embrace your preferences, savor every sip, and all will indeed be well.

MEAT GUIDE

When you're in the market for meat, understanding certain aspects such as grading, aging, purchasing, and storage can elevate your culinary experience by ensuring you always pick the finest cuts.

Grading:

Ever wonder what those quality grades on meat mean? They're essentially your guide to the meat's attributes, like tenderness, juiciness, and flavor. These grades factor in the animal's age, the meat's hue, texture, and marbling level.

Here are the US Department of Agriculture (USDA) grades:

Beef:
USDA Prime, Choice, Select, Standard, Commercial, Utility, Cutter, and Canner

Veal:
USDA Prime, Choice, Good, Standard, Utility

Lamb:
USDA Prime, Choice, Good, Utility

Pork:
USDA No. 1, No. 2, No. 3, Utility

A brief insight into two primary grades:

USDA Prime Meats: Primarily reserved for elite venues like top-notch restaurants and gourmet markets, these cuts are richly marbled with a generous layer of fat.

USDA Choice Meats: These are more common and are the favorites in quality food establishments and grocery stores. They have prominent marbling, though less fat than Prime, and promise a tender, juicy outcome.

Meats like USDA Select or Standard for beef, and USDA Good for lamb and veal, might not be as tender or flavorful as the top grades, but they're still popular in many outlets. The term "no roll" signifies beef that hasn't been grade stamped by a USDA inspector. A significant portion of retail beef in the U.S. is "no roll," but if graded, would be categorized as USDA Select.

Aging of Beef:

Aging can be accomplished in two ways—wet and dry.

Wet Aging: This involves storing meats in vacuum-sealed packaging under refrigeration for up to six weeks. This process allows natural enzymes and microorganisms to break down the connective tissues, thus tenderizing and enhancing the flavor of the meat. Upon opening, there might be a fleeting off-putting odor, but it dissipates quickly.

Dry Aging: Here, meats are stored in controlled temperature, humidity, and airflow for a similar duration. This is essentially the initial stage of natural decomposition. The moisture evaporation in dry aging can result in a weight loss of 5-20%. The formation of mold can add to the flavor profile, although it needs trimming later. Because of the moisture loss and trimming, dry-aged meats can be pricier and are often found in specialty stores.

Purchasing Tips: Ensure you buy meat in quantities that your refrigerator and freezer can handle. If you're planning on freezing the meat, opt for higher-end cuts to maintain the quality and marbling.

Storage Essentials:
Meat is perishable. Fresh meats should ideally be stored between 30 and 35°F (-1 and 2°C). Keep vacuum-sealed meats in their packaging until use. Those with an unbroken seal last three to four weeks under appropriate refrigeration. For non-vacuum packed meats, loosely wrapping or using air-permeable paper is best. Avoid tightly wrapping with plastic as it encourages bacterial growth. When freezing, quicker is better to avoid ice crystals. The optimal temperature for frozen meat is 50°F (-45°C). Handled correctly, meats can be frozen up to six months. Always thaw frozen meats in the refrigerator, not at room temperature or in warm water.

THE EARLY YEARS

In our opening chapter, we journey back to the formative years of my culinary adventure. While my experience was nascent, it didn't dictate that my dishes would lack zest. The recipes shared here are not just relics of my past; they are timeless staples that continually grace my kitchen. Just as our parents lay the foundation during our toddler years that we build upon throughout life, so too do the initial recipes and techniques in our culinary repertoire. Let's embark on this flavorful journey.

TANGY BBQ SAUCE

12 cups fresh brewed coffee, reduced to 6 cups

¼ teaspoon kosher salt

1 teaspoon black pepper

1 garlic clove, minced

1 teaspoon onion powder

3 dashes hot sauce

⅓ cup cola

¼ cup honey

1 teaspoon sugar

2 tablespoons chili powder

½ teaspoon Dijon mustard

In a medium saucepot, mix reduced coffee, salt, garlic, and chili powder.

Simmer for 5 minutes.

In a separate bowl, merge the remaining ingredients.

Whisk together all ingredients in the saucepot and let simmer for 20 minutes, or until it thickens enough to coat a spoon.

CUBANO PIE

1 cup shredded cooked pork

1 cup grated Swiss cheese

1 cup grated mozzarella cheese

2 cups chopped smoked ham

2 garlic cloves, minced

¼ sweet onion, finely diced

1 jalapeño, minced

2 Roma tomatoes, diced

1 green bell pepper, seeded and diced

2 cups heavy cream

1 cup grated Parmesan cheese

1 tablespoon grain mustard

2 pie crusts

Sauce:

1 ½ cups sour cream

2 tablespoons lime juice

2 tablespoons fresh orange juice

1 teaspoon kosher salt

1 teaspoon black pepper

1 teaspoon fresh or dried oregano

Sauté garlic, onion, tomatoes, jalapeño, and bell peppers in a large skillet until softened.

In a mixing bowl, combine heavy cream, Parmesan, and mustard. Set aside.

Pre-bake the bottom pie crust in an 8" pie pan at 350 degrees until golden.

Layer Swiss, pork, sautéed veggies, mozzarella, and ham in the pre-baked crust.

Pour the cream mixture on top and seal with the second crust. Bake at 350 degrees until golden brown on top.

Rest for 10 minutes and serve with sauce.

BRAISED CHICKEN THIGHS WITH ROASTED FINGERLING POTATOES

2 tablespoons all-purpose flour

2 teaspoons paprika

1 teaspoon kosher salt

2 sprigs fresh thyme

2 sprigs fresh oregano

½ teaspoon black pepper

1 ½ cups carrots, sliced

1 ½ cups celery, diced

1 ½ pounds cipollini or pearl onions, peeled

½ fennel bulb

5 garlic cloves, smashed

8 chicken thighs

1 tablespoon extra-virgin olive oil

1 ½ cups chicken stock

½ cup dry white wine

1 ½ pounds fingerling potatoes, halved

Heat oil in a pot or Dutch oven over medium heat.

Season chicken with salt, pepper, paprika, and flour, then brown all sides in the pot. Set aside.

Sauté veggies, thyme, and oregano in pot drippings.

Deglaze with wine, add stock and bring to boil.

Reduce heat, add chicken, and cover to simmer for 35 minutes.

Season potatoes with salt, pepper, and olive oil.

Roast at 375 degrees until tender and serve with braised chicken.

SPINACH ARTICHOKE DIP

1 garlic clove, chopped

5 ounces frozen spinach, thawed and drained

3 ounces artichoke hearts, drained/ chopped

2 ½ ounces mozzarella, grated

2 ½ ounces cheddar, grated

8 ounces cream cheese

2 ounces milk

2 ounces heavy cream

½ teaspoon onion powder

½ teaspoon garlic powder

1 round loaf, hollowed

Sauté spinach, garlic, and artichokes in a heavy saucepot. Introduce cream cheese until melted, followed by liquids.

Add seasoning and half the grated cheese.

Pour into a pre-toasted hollowed bread bowl, top with remaining cheese and bake at 350 degrees for a bubbly finish.

Tip: For a crisp bread bowl, toast the hollowed loaf at 350 degrees for 5-8 minutes.

SAUTÉED MIXED VEGETABLES

2 tablespoons extra-virgin olive oil

1 cup green beans, blanched

1 cup zucchini, julienned

½ fennel bulb, sliced

1 cup each of red and yellow bell peppers, julienned

1 garlic clove, minced

salt and pepper, to taste

Blanch green beans in boiling salted water for 3-5 minutes, then cool in an ice bath.

In a sauté pan, heat oil with garlic. Add all vegetables and sauté for roughly 7 minutes. Season to taste.

Tip: When preparing fennel, trim and set aside the fronds. After halving the bulb, remove the core before slicing.

ROASTED POTATOES

1 ½ pounds fingerling potatoes

1 ounce olive oil

1 garlic clove, minced

1 sprig rosemary, finely chopped

1 sprig thyme, finely chopped

salt and pepper, to taste

Wash the potatoes and cut them in half lengthwise. In a mixing bowl, toss the potatoes with olive oil, minced garlic, chopped rosemary, and thyme. Spread them out on a baking sheet in a single layer. Season with salt and pepper.

Roast in a 400-degreee preheated oven until golden brown and tender.

Tip: Tossing the potatoes occasionally ensures even roasting and prevents them from sticking to the pan.

BAKED ACORN SQUASH

1 acorn squash, halved

2 ounces unsalted butter, melted

1 ounce brown sugar

4 ounces fresh-squeezed orange juice

salt and pepper, to taste

Preheat oven to 350 degrees.

Halve the acorn squash and remove seeds and strings.

Place the halves cut side down on a baking sheet and bake until tender.

Turn the halves cut side up and pierce the flesh multiple times with a fork.

Equally distribute the butter, brown sugar, and orange juice among the squash halves.

Continue baking until the squash is very tender.

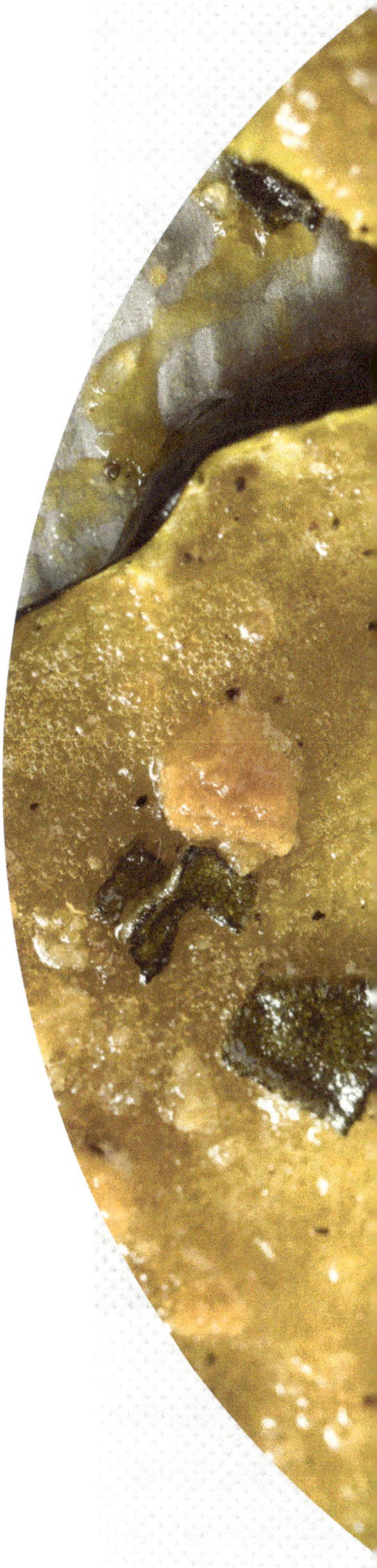

JALAPEÑO CORN BREAD

6 ounces cornmeal (about ¾ cup)

1 tablespoon sugar

1 teaspoon baking powder

1 teaspoon salt

6 ounces buttermilk

2 eggs, lightly beaten

2 ounces oil

4 ounces fresh corn kernels

1 roasted, peeled, and seeded poblano pepper

1 roasted and peeled jalapeño

Preheat the oven to 375 degrees and grease your preferred baking pan.

In a large mixing bowl, combine cornmeal, sugar, baking powder, and salt.

In another bowl, whisk the buttermilk and eggs together.

Mix the wet ingredients into the dry, then stir in the oil, corn, and peppers.

Pour batter into the prepared pan and bake until golden brown and a tester inserted comes out clean, roughly 30 minutes.

MUSHROOM CEVICHE

1 pound mushrooms, cleaned

Dressing:

1 ounce lemon juice

1 ounce lime juice

1 ounce orange juice

1 ounce olive oil

1 ounce red onion, finely diced

1 ounce red bell pepper, finely diced

1 garlic clove, minced

½ ounce cilantro, chopped

salt and pepper, to taste

Clean mushrooms and cut into quarters.

In a mixing bowl, combine all the dressing ingredients.

Add the mushrooms to the dressing and stir to coat.

Refrigerate for at least 1 hour before serving.

Serving Suggestions: Serve with tortilla chips, fried plantains, as a side to grilled seafood, or mix into pasta for a veggie main dish.

ARROZ A LA MEXICANA

1 ounce olive oil

2 ounces onion, finely diced

1 garlic clove, minced

1 cup rice

2 ounces carrots, finely diced

6 ounces tomatoes, concassé

2 cups prepared chicken stock

1 bay leaf

salt and pepper, to taste

In a pot, heat olive oil over medium heat. Add rice, onion, and garlic.

Sauté until the rice is lightly browned, giving off a nutty aroma.

Mix in the carrots, tomatoes, bay leaf, chicken stock, and season with salt and pepper.

Bring the mixture to a simmer, then reduce the heat to low and cover. Let it simmer for approximately 20 minutes.

Fluff the cooked rice gently with a fork and serve.

BRUSSELS SPROUTS

1 pound Brussels sprouts, trimmed

2 ounces butter

1 ounce onion, diced

1 ounce bacon, diced

Boil the Brussels sprouts in salted water for 20-30 minutes or until tender. Drain and cool.

In a sauté pan, melt butter over medium heat. Add bacon and onion, and sauté until softened.

Incorporate the parboiled Brussels sprouts and continue to sauté until tender and slightly browned.

OATMEAL PANCAKES

1 cup all-purpose flour

1 cup rolled oats

1 teaspoon baking powder

1 teaspoon baking soda

¼ cup walnuts, toasted and chopped

¼ cup raisins

2 whole eggs

2 bananas, mashed

¼ cup vegetable oil

1 teaspoon cinnamon

1 teaspoon vanilla extract

Sift together the flour, baking powder, baking soda, and set aside.

In another bowl, combine the mashed bananas, eggs, vegetable oil, cinnamon, and vanilla extract.

Gradually mix the dry ingredients into the wet until fully combined, ensuring no lumps remain.

Preheat a griddle over medium heat. Pour batter to form pancakes and cook for 2-3 minutes on each side or until golden brown.

Toasting Tip: To toast the walnuts, heat a dry skillet over medium heat. Add walnuts and stir frequently for 2-3 minutes until they're fragrant and lightly browned.

CAST-IRON FLATBREAD

1 ¼ cup all-purpose flour, sifted

½ tablespoon baking powder

½ teaspoon salt

¼ teaspoon sugar

1 cup warm water

¼ cup olive oil

1 tablespoon onion powder

In a mixing bowl, combine flour, baking powder, salt, sugar, and onion powder. Mix using a dough hook attachment on low for 3-4 minutes.

Gradually add warm water to the mixture until the dough is sticky. Remove the dough from the bowl and divide into balls roughly the size of a 50-cent piece.

Flatten each ball into a 4-inch round. Fry in a cast-iron pan with olive oil over medium heat until golden on each side.

MIXED GREEN SALAD WITH CITRUS VINAIGRETTE

8 ounces mixed greens, washed and dried

1 ounce fresh orange juice

1 ounce honey

3 ounces apple cider vinegar

5 ounces olive oil

In a serving bowl, whisk together the orange juice, honey, and apple cider vinegar.

Gradually drizzle in the olive oil while whisking to emulsify the dressing.

Before serving, toss the mixed greens in the vinaigrette until lightly coated.

BLACK BEAN BURRITOS WITH AVOCADO

½ cup diced peeled avocado

1 teaspoon fresh lime juice

1 teaspoon olive oil

2 cloves garlic, minced

¼ cup water

2 teaspoon ground cumin

2 (15 ounce) cans black beans, drained

4 (10 inch) flour tortillas

6 tablespoon fat-free sour cream

6 teaspoon bottled salsa

Mix avocado and lime juice to coat.

In a medium saucepan, heat oil over medium-high heat. Sauté garlic for 1 minute.

Add water, cumin, and beans. Simmer for 3 minutes or until heated through.

Warm tortillas as per package instructions.

Add ¼ cup bean mixture to each tortilla. Top with sour cream, salsa, and avocado. Roll to close.

GREEK-FLAVORED TURKEY BURGERS

1 large egg white

1 cup chopped red onion

¾ cup chopped fresh mint

½ cup dry breadcrumbs

⅓ cup crumbled feta cheese (about 1 ½ ounces)

2 tablespoon fresh lemon juice

1 teaspoon fresh dill

1 pound ground turkey

Cooking spray

4 (1 ½ ounces) hamburger buns, split

1 (7 ounces) bottle roasted red bell peppers, sliced

In a large bowl, lightly beat egg white. Add onion and the next 6 ingredients, mixing well.

Shape mixture into 4 patties, each ½ inch thick.

In a skillet over medium-high heat, cook patties for 8 minutes per side or until done.

Assemble burgers with peppers on buns.

Tip: For freezing, wrap uncooked patties in plastic wrap and foil. Freeze for up to 2 months. Thaw in the fridge before cooking.

Substitutions: Replace ground turkey with 85/15 lean ground beef, a mix of beef and lamb, or solely ground lamb.

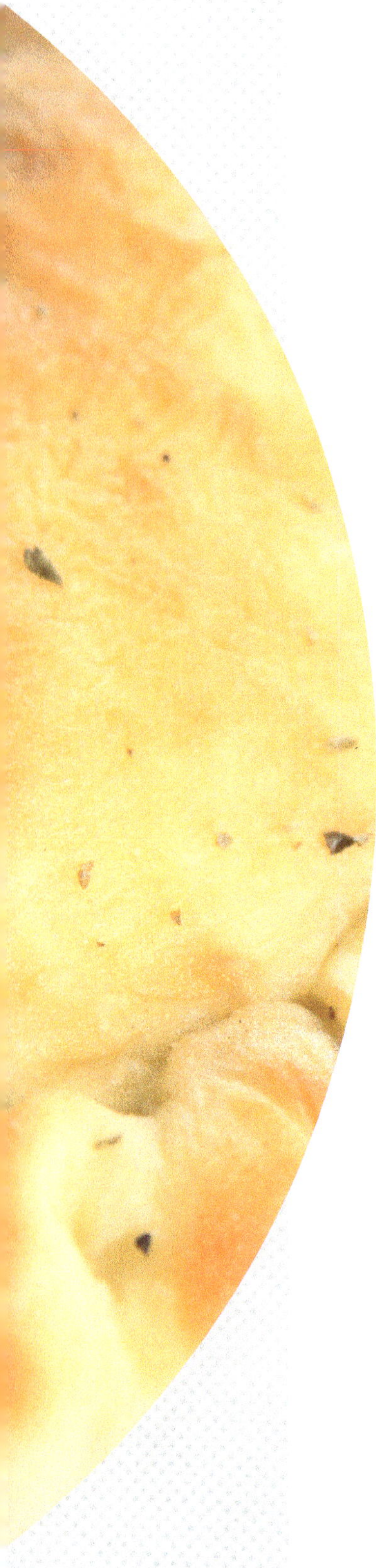

HAM, SPINACH, AND SUN-DRIED TOMATO CALZONES

1 cup part-skim ricotta

¾ cup shredded part-skim mozzarella cheese

¼ cup grated Parmesan cheese

1 teaspoon dried basil

½ teaspoon crushed fennel seed

¼ teaspoon black pepper

1 (10 ounce) package frozen chopped spinach, thawed and drained

3 ounces lean ham, chopped

6 oil-packed sun-dried tomato halves, chopped

1 (13.8 ounce) can pizza crust dough

cooking spray

Preheat oven to 450 degrees.

Mix the first 9 ingredients together.

Divide dough into 5 pieces and shape into 5-inch circles.

Place ½ cup of the spinach mixture on half of each dough circle, fold and crimp edges.

Place on a baking sheet and bake for 14 minutes or until browned.

CHICKEN SAUSAGE AND PROVOLONE PENNE BAKE

1 pound uncooked penne

1 tablespoon olive oil

¾ cup chopped red bell pepper

1 (12 ounce) package sweet basil and pine nut chicken sausage, sliced

2 cloves garlic, minced

1 tablespoon tomato paste

1 tablespoon balsamic vinegar

½ teaspoon salt

¼ teaspoon dried oregano

¼ teaspoon crushed red pepper

3 (14.4 ounce) cans diced tomatoes, undrained

1 cup shredded sharp provolone cheese

1 cup grated fresh Parmesan cheese

cooking spray

Cook penne as directed on the package.

Preheat oven to 350 degrees.

In a large skillet, heat oil and sauté onion, bell pepper, sausage, and garlic for 5 minutes.

Add tomato paste, vinegar, salt, oregano, red pepper, and tomatoes. Simmer for 15 minutes.

Mix pasta and sauce, then transfer to a baking dish. Top with cheeses. Bake for 25 minutes or until bubbly.

THE
MIDDLE
AGES

Welcome to a time reminiscent of the Middle Ages, an era where imagination sprouted and creativity unfurled its wings. In this chapter of my culinary journey, my approach to food began to evolve. I began to liberate myself from the confines of store-bought staples and ventured into crafting dishes entirely from scratch.

With my grandmother's guidance, her presence was like the soft touch of a master artist refining a canvas. She gradually nudged me toward crafting my signature – simple dishes, yet imbued with audacious and unconventional spices and flavors. While her physical involvement dwindled, she was subtly preparing me to stand alone in the kitchen.

Life, in its intricate ways, mirrors this journey. As we mature, we yearn for the liberty to sculpt our identity and style. I deeply believe that everything we do should be an echo of our soul, and cooking is no exception. There's truth in the adage that one's culinary choices are a window into their essence. As I've often remarked, the dishes you create and the food you savor reveal volumes about who you are.

TROPICAL SALSA

1 avocado, diced

½ pineapple, peeled, cored, and diced

½ papaya, peeled, seeded, and diced

1 lime, zested and juiced

1 lemon, zested and juiced

¼ cup honey

1 pinch kosher salt

In a mixing bowl, whisk together honey, lemon and lime juice.

Add the fruit, lemon zest, lime zest, and salt to the bowl and toss.

Once tossed, chill until you're ready to serve.

Tips: When working with avocado, avoid handling it too much. This will help ensure it doesn't break down. Also, dice the avocado right before serving the salsa to maintain its color and texture.

Serving Suggestions: This salsa pairs beautifully with grilled shrimp, fish, or chicken. It can also be served with pita chips or plantain chips for a Caribbean flair. If your fruit isn't ripe, you can add a bit of sugar.

CRAB SALAD

1 cup homemade mayonnaise (page 92)

2 tablespoons Dijon mustard

2 tablespoons lemon juice

2 tablespoons lemon zest

1 teaspoon cracked black pepper

¼ teaspoon Kosher salt

½ teaspoon minced garlic

⅛ cup chopped parsley

¼ teaspoon onion powder

3 Roma tomatoes, peeled and diced

2 asparagus stalks, diced

1 ½ cups jumbo lump crab, cleaned

Fill a large sauce pot half full with water then bring to a boil. Once it comes to a rolling boil, add Kosher salt.

Add asparagus and blanch for two minutes. Remove asparagus from boiling water and shock in an ice bath. Once cool, remove from ice bath and dry on paper towel.

In a mixing bowl, combine mayonnaise, Dijon mustard, lemon juice, lemon zest, seasoning and parsley. Whisk together and gently fold in crab, tomato and asparagus.

Serving Suggestions: Serve in a chilled martini glass with bibb or butter lettuce on bottom and crab salad on top.

Fry wonton wrappers in oil to resemble taco shells for a crab salad taco.

Tip: An ice bath is a bowl filled with ice and cold water used to quickly cool and preserve the color of blanched vegetables.

ASPARAGUS FRITTATA

6 each large eggs

¼ cup chopped Italian parsley

2 tablespoons heavy cream

½ teaspoon black pepper

1 tablespoon extra virgin olive oil

1 pound fresh asparagus, trimmed and cut into ¼ inch pieces

⅓ cup crème fraiche or sour cream

½ cup chives, minced

¼ cup Parmesan cheese

¼ cup gruyere cheese

½ teaspoon kosher salt

¼ teaspoon freshly grated nutmeg

¼ each yellow onion, minced

1 tablespoon unsalted butter

Preheat broiler.

Whisk eggs, ¼ of the chives, parsley, parmesan cheese, gruyere cheese, heavy cream, salt, pepper, and nutmeg until blended.

In a nonstick skillet over medium heat, melt butter and olive oil. Once heated, add asparagus and onion and sauté until tender, about 4 minutes.

Pour the egg mixture over asparagus and reduce heat to low. Cook until edges are just set, about 3 minutes.Using a heatproof spatula, lift the cooked edges of the mixture and tilt the pan, allowing uncooked egg to flow beneath.Continue cooking until the top of t he mixture is nearly set, about 5 more minutes.

Place the skillet under the broiler until the mixture puffs up and is lightly golden on top, approximately 2 minutes. Serve hot.

FLANK STEAK WRAP
WITH CARAMELIZED ONIONS & BLEU CHEESE

1 teaspoon kosher salt

½ teaspoon black pepper

2 garlic cloves, minced

¼ cup extra virgin olive oil

1 teaspoon red pepper flakes

1 pound flank steak, trimmed

6 cups sliced white onions

½ cup crumbled bleu cheese

¼ cup mayonnaise

2 20-inch tortillas

Season meat with oil, pepper, garlic, and salt. Cover and chill for at least 2 hours or overnight.

Cook steak on a preheated grill to desired doneness.

Once cooked, remove from grill, cover with foil and allow meat to rest so the juices may redistribute, about 10 minutes.

Cut the steak diagonally across the grain into thin slices.

In a sauté pan, cook onions over medium-high heat until they are a rich golden color, about 10-15 minutes, stirring often.

In a small bowl, combine bleu cheese and mayo.

Spread 2 tablespoons of the bleu cheese onto a warmed tortilla. Then top with 3 ounces of steak and ½ cup of caramelized onions.

Roll then cut in half.

Tip: Letting the steak rest allows the juices to stay in the steak, resulting in a more flavorful steak.

Serving Suggestions: Can also be served as a salad instead of a wrap using salad greens.

BROCCOLI AND CHEESE STUFFED POTATOES

2 large baking potatoes (Idaho or Russet)

2 slices bacon or pancetta

1 cup fresh or frozen broccoli florets

1 cup sliced button mushrooms

½ cup chopped yellow onion

1 garlic clove, minced

½ cup grated Swiss cheese

¼ cup grated cheddar cheese

¼ cup sour cream

2 tablespoons heavy cream

½ teaspoon black pepper

⅛ teaspoon kosher salt

pinch nutmeg

Rinse, dry, and pierce each potato with a fork. Wrap each potato in foil and bake for 18-25 minutes.

While potatoes are baking, heat a large nonstick skillet on medium heat. Cook bacon until crisp then remove from pan.

In that skillet, sauté onion, garlic, and mushrooms until translucent.

Add broccoli and heat through until tender. Remove from heat.

Cut each potato in half lengthwise. Scoop out the pulp from the potato, leaving a ¼ inch of the inside in the potato.

Combine the potato pulp, broccoli mixture, cheeses, and remaining ingredients.

Divide the mixture between the four shells.

Bake at 450 degrees for 8 minutes or until the potatoes are thoroughly heated.

Sprinkle the top of the potatoes with the crumbled bacon.

BOLOGNESE

3 tablespoons extra virgin olive oil

6 tablespoons chopped red onion

6 tablespoons chopped red & yellow bell pepper

6 tablespoons finely chopped celery

6 tablespoons finely chopped carrot

3 tablespoons chopped capers

6 tablespoons chopped garlic

1 sprig each of rosemary, thyme, and basil

½ pound ground veal

½ pound ground beef

½ cup dry red wine (Chianti)

½ cup white wine

16 ounces canned tomatoes (San Marzano preferably), pureed

kosher salt and black pepper to taste

Heat a heavy-bottomed sauce pot or Dutch oven over medium-high heat. Add olive oil, then add onions and sauté until they are opaque.

Once onions are opaque, add carrots, celery, capers, and sauté until tender. Add garlic, bell peppers, ground veal, and ground beef.

Once meat has browned, deglaze with wine then add pureed tomatoes, herbs, salt, and pepper.

Simmer for 30-40 minutes on low heat.

Tip: Stir periodically to prevent the sauce from sticking.

Serving Suggestions: This sauce is versatile. While it's best known for lasagna, it can also be used as a topping for stuffed bell peppers.

STUFFED MUSHROOMS

10 button or cremini mushrooms, stemmed

6 ounces panko breadcrumbs

½ ounce oregano

½ ounce basil

8 ounces cream cheese, softened

1 egg

1 ounce Parmesan cheese, grated

Combine 5 ounces of breadcrumbs, herbs, egg, and softened cream cheese.

Place the mushroom caps side down on a sheet pan and bake at 400 degrees for five minutes.

Remove the mushrooms from the oven and let them cool.

Once cooled, stuff the mushrooms with the filling, top with remaining breadcrumbs and parmesan, and bake for five more minutes.

Serving Suggestions: This recipe can be transformed into a vegetarian entrée by using a portabella mushroom instead.

MONTERREY JACK AND ROASTED CHILI POLENTA

5 ounces chicken stock

5 ounces milk

1 ounce unsalted butter

1 teaspoon granulated sugar

½ teaspoon kosher salt

3 ounces polenta

2 ounces Monterrey Jack cheese, grated

1 poblano pepper, roasted, peeled, seeded, and diced

In a medium sauce pot, bring the chicken stock to a boil.

Reduce heat to a simmer and stir in milk, butter, sugar, and salt.

Slowly add in the polenta in a thin stream, whisking constantly.

Lower heat and continue stirring for 10-20 minutes or until it thickens.

Once thickened, stir in cheese and peppers.

Continue to cook over low heat until the mixture falls away easily from the sides of the pan.

Season with salt and pepper and serve immediately.

Tip: For a vegetarian option, substitute chicken stock with vegetable stock.

Serving Suggestions: This polenta pairs perfectly with grilled meats or mole.

HONEY ROASTED BUTTERNUT SQUASH AND TURNIPS

12 ounces butternut squash, peeled & seeded

6 ounces turnips, peeled

2 ounces honey

½ ounce olive oil

1 bunch tarragon, minced

Cut butternut squash and turnips into 1-inch cubes. Toss in seasoning.

Roast at 375°F on an oiled sheet pan for 30 minutes.

Tip: Make sure to loosen the vegetables with a spatula periodically to prevent them from sticking to the pan.

Serving Suggestions: Serve the vegetables on a platter, drizzled with balsamic vinegar.

GLAZED TURNIPS

1 pound turnips, peeled

1 ounce butter

1 ½ ounces maple syrup

salt and pepper to taste

¼ teaspoon nutmeg

¼ teaspoon cinnamon

parsley for garnish

Slice the turnips into short batonettes.

In a pot, parboil the turnips until they are tender.

Drain the water and set them aside.

In a sauté pan, melt the butter, then stir in the sugar.

Bring the mixture to a simmer.

Add the parboiled turnips to the pan.

Gently toss the turnips in the butter-sugar mixture until they are nicely glazed.

Taste and adjust the seasoning as needed.

Finish by garnishing with freshly chopped parsley.

VEGETABLE TEMPURA

12 ounces sweet potatoes, peeled and cut into julienne

1 Japanese eggplant, cut lengthwise ¼-inch into 4 slices

4 mushrooms, sliced lengthwise ¼-inch thickness

1 zucchini, sliced lengthwise into ¼-inch thickness

For Tempura Batter:

(Prepare 15 minutes ahead)

½ cup cornstarch

½ cup all purpose flour

1 egg

½ tsp salt

½ cup cold water

oil for frying as needed

Stir batter ingredients together. Avoid over stirring; the batter should remain lumpy.

Heat oil to 375 degrees.

Dip julienne strips into batter.

Fry until light golden brown and drain on paper towels.

Dip the remaining vegetables in batter and fry.

Serve with tempura dipping sauce.

Tempura Dipping Sauce:

¼ cup Mirin

¼ cup soy sauce

1 cup dashi

1 tablespoon granulated sugar

Mix all ingredients together.

HONEY ROASTED BUTTERNUT SQUASH WITH TURNIPS AND PARSNIPS

6 ounces butternut squash, peeled, seeded, cubed

12 ounces turnips, peeled and cubed

2 parsnips, peeled and cut

2 ounces honey

1 tablespoon fresh thyme

½ tablespoon fresh tarragon

1 dry bay leaf

2 cloves garlic, minced

½ ounce extra virgin olive oil

1 cup breadcrumbs, seasoned and prepared

1 tablespoon chives

Cut butternut squash and turnips into 1-inch cubes.

Toss butternut, turnips, and parsnips with honey, oil, and seasonings.

Place on a lightly oiled sheet pan.

Roast at 375 degrees for 30 minutes.

Toss with breadcrumbs, chives, and 1 tbsp of butter, then serve.

FRENCH ONION SOUP

1 pound white onions, sliced

16 ounces vegetable stock

1 baguette, sliced

14 ounces Gruyere cheese, grated

kosher salt and black pepper to taste

1 bay leaf

Caramelize onions on medium heat, stirring occasionally.

Once caramelized, add bay leaf and stock, then simmer on low for 30-45 minutes.

Toast the bread slices under the broiler.

Place soup in oven-safe soup crocks, ladle in the soup, top with a crouton, and cover with grated gruyere.

Broil just to melt the cheese.

Serve immediately.

TERIYAKI MEAT SKEWERS

8 ounces beef top round, sliced 2" long and ranging from 2"-½"-¼" in thickness

2 ounces soy sauce

1 ½ tablespoons brown sugar

1 ½ tablespoon sherry

1 teaspoon minced ginger root

1 garlic clove, minced

12 bamboo skewers, soaked in water

Combine soy sauce, sugar, sherry, ginger, and garlic. Stir on low heat until sugar is dissolved.

Marinate the meat slices in the soy mixture for 30 minutes.

Thread meat onto skewers and grill until done.

TALL AND FLUFFY BUTTERMILK BISCUITS

1 cup unbleached all-purpose flour

1 tablespoon double-acting baking powder

1 tablespoon sugar

1 teaspoon salt

½ teaspoon baking soda

4 tablespoon cold, unsalted butter, cut into ¼ inch cubes

1 ½ cups cold buttermilk, preferably low-fat

To form and finish biscuits:

1 cup unbleached all-purpose flour (for dusting)

2 tablespoon unsalted butter, melted

Adjust oven rack to the middle and preheat to 500 degrees. Spray a 9-inch round cake pan with nonstick cooking spray.

For the dough, combine flour, baking powder, sugar, salt, and baking soda in a food processor. Add butter and pulse until the mixture looks like coarse cornmeal.

Transfer to a bowl, add buttermilk, and stir until just combined.

Drop scoops of dough into the flour on a baking sheet, then shape into balls and place in the cake pan.

Brush the biscuits with melted butter, reduce oven to 450 degrees, and bake until deep golden brown (about 15 more minutes).

Remove, cool slightly, and serve.

THE REBEL YEARS

Just as children experience a phase of rebellion, so did my culinary journey. As I delved deeper into my culinary education, I grappled with the rigidity of traditional methods. While my primary focus was on pastry, I wasn't spared from the conventional culinary classes. It was there that I observed a prevalent close-mindedness among many peers.

Classic techniques have their merits, but there's always room for evolution to enhance flavors, textures, and presentations. Driven by this belief, I immersed myself in global cuisines, aiming to refine my pastry skills through diverse inspirations. The recipes that follow are a testament to a phase where I embraced unbounded creativity, urging you to re-imagine the very essence of food.

RED ONION MARMALADE

1 red onion

1 kiwi, peeled and minced

Juice of 1 lime

3 garlic cloves, minced

½ ginger root, peeled and minced

3 serrano peppers, minced

¼ cup honey

4 tablespoons granulated sugar

½ cup red wine vinegar

In a small saucepan, sweat the onion until soft and translucent.

Add the kiwi, lime juice, and garlic, and simmer for 10 minutes.

Add the ginger, serrano pepper, and honey, then sauté until it reaches a jam-like consistency.

Stir in the sugar and deglaze with red wine vinegar.

Simmer for an additional 10 minutes, then remove from heat.

Tips: Kiwi can be omitted if not in season. For garlic, if you're not adept at mincing, you can grate it using a grater. Be cautious not to grate your fingers.

Serving Suggestions: This marmalade is ideal for enhancing burgers and sandwiches. Try it on grilled bread with goat cheese and honey for a delightful appetizer.

STUFFED FIGS

5 fresh figs, cut in half

2 ½ ounces bleu cheese, crumbled

2 ½ ounces honey

Split the figs in half. Using a melon baller, scoop out a portion of the center from each fig.

Stuff each fig with ¼ ounce of bleu cheese.

Drizzle with honey.

Tips: Exercise caution when hollowing out the figs to prevent breaking. For added flavor, consider grilling the figs before proceeding with the recipe. **Substitutions:** If figs are unavailable, peaches are an excellent alternative.

Serving Suggestions: Present on a platter alongside salad greens and salamis for an ideal antipasto, or serve them standalone.

BACON BRAISED BRUSSELS SPROUTS

1 pound brussels sprouts, trimmed

1 ½ ounces unsalted butter

1 ounce onion, diced

2 cloves garlic, minced

1 pinch crushed pepper flakes

2 ounces bacon or pancetta

6 ounces vegetable or chicken stock

1 bay leaf

Heat butter in a sauté pan. Add onions, bacon, bay leaf, garlic, and pepper flakes. Let sauté.

Add brussels sprouts and sauté for 10 minutes.

Season with salt and pepper. Add stock and braise until tender.

Tips: To trim the brussels sprouts, simply remove the bottom core and the outer set of leaves. For a vegetarian version, omit the pancetta and use vegetable stock.

FLANK STEAK BRUSCHETTA

14 ounces flank steak, trimmed

1 baguette, sliced at an angle

½ ounce rosemary

½ ounce oregano

kosher salt and black pepper, to taste

½ ounce extra virgin olive oil

1 tomato, diced

1 bunch basil, chopped

Season the flank steak and rub with olive oil. Let it sit for five minutes.

Grill the baguette slices until both sides are golden brown.

Grill the steak to your preferred level of doneness. Allow the steak to rest for five minutes before slicing thinly.

Rub one side of each baguette slice with a halved garlic clove.

Top the baguette with the steak slices, diced tomato, and chopped basil. Drizzle with olive oil and serve.

PASTA ALLA CARBONARA

4 ounces pancetta or bacon

2 egg yolks

½ cup heavy cream

2 ounces Parmesan cheese

½ cup reserved pasta water

½ pound tagliatelle

kosher salt and black pepper, to taste

pinch of nutmeg

Sauté the pancetta or bacon until crisp. Remove and set aside.

Cook the pasta in boiling salted water.

Combine the egg yolks, heavy cream, and Parmesan cheese.

Heat the fat in the pan, add the pasta and cream mixture, and cook over low heat until sauce thickens. If needed, incorporate the reserved pasta water to reach the desired consistency.
Season to taste and serve immediately.

Tips: Prepare this pasta right before serving. The sauce doesn't reheat well. After boiling the pasta, simply drain without rinsing.

FRESH TOMATO SAUCE

2 ounces clarified butter

8 ounces onions, diced

2 cloves garlic, minced

48 ounces tomato concassee, peeled, seeded, diced

4 ounces tomato paste

salt and pepper to taste

1 tablespoon basil, chopped

1 tablespoon parsley, chopped

Sweat the onions and garlic in clarified butter until translucent.

Add the tomato concassee and tomato paste; simmer for 29 minutes until desired consistency.

Adjust seasoning and add herbs.

Tips: To prepare the tomato concassee: mark a cross on the top of the tomatoes, blanch in boiling water, chill in an ice bath, peel, deseed, and dice.

BUTTERED NOODLES

3 cups all-purpose flour

5 whole eggs

15 ounces olive oil

¼ teaspoon salt

butter, as needed

Place flour in a mixing bowl with a dough hook.

In a separate bowl, mix the wet ingredients.

Combine the wet and dry ingredients until dough forms. Wrap and refrigerate for 30 minutes.

Roll out the dough using a pasta machine, starting at the thickest setting and progressively thinning it out, dusting with flour as necessary. Slice the dough into ½-inch wide noodles and let them dry.

Boil the noodles in salted water until al dente and drain.

In a sauté pan, melt and lightly brown the butter.

Toss the noodles in the butter until well coated. Serve immediately.

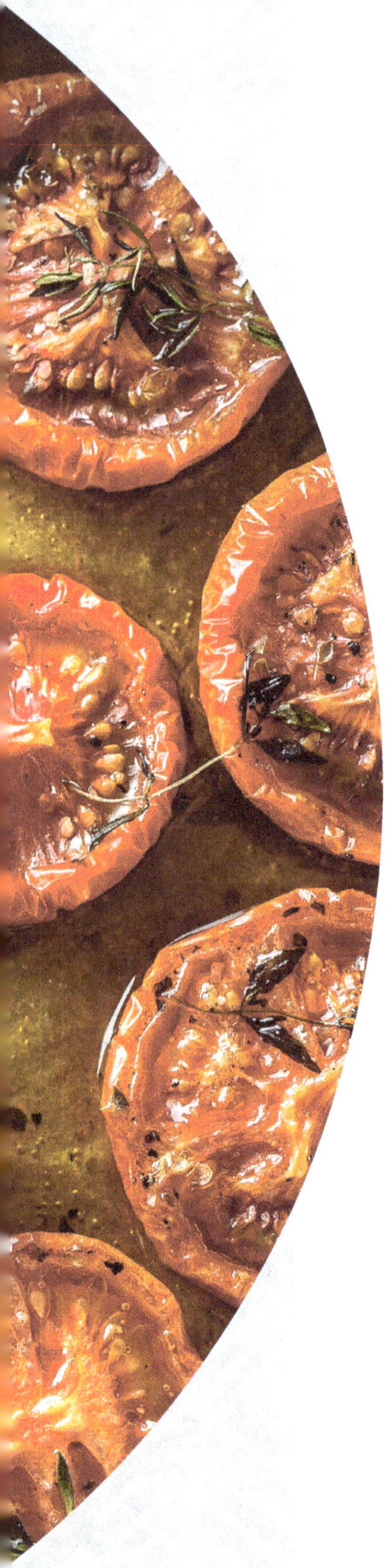

BROILED TOMATOES

2 ounces clarified butter

1 ounce onion, finely diced

1 clove garlic

2 ounces Japanese breadcrumbs

½ ounce Parmesan cheese

1 teaspoon parsley, chopped

salt and pepper to taste

2 beefsteak tomatoes, halved

Heat sauté pan with butter, add onions and garlic, and sweat until translucent. Transfer to a bowl.

Mix breadcrumbs, parmesan cheese, and parsley. Season.

Prep tomatoes, season cut side, and top each with breadcrumb mixture.

Bake at 350 degrees until hot.

SUMMER SQUASH NOODLES

½ pound yellow squash, long julienne

½ pound zucchini, long julienne

¼ pound leeks, long julienne

1 ounce butter

1 teaspoon lemon zest

salt and pepper to taste

herbs, chopped

Melt butter in a sauté pan, add leeks, and sweat.

Add zucchini and squash, sautéing until tender. Season and garnish with herbs.

Tip: Consider adding julienned roasted red bell peppers.

GLAZED BEETS

1 pound beets, whole

1 ounce unsalted butter

½ ounce lemon juice

2 ounces sugar, honey, or maple syrup

salt and pepper to taste

Boil and peel the beets, then cut into wedges.

In a sauté pan, melt butter, add lemon juice and sweetener, and simmer with beets until glazed.

BRAISED SHORT RIBS

2 pounds beef short ribs

flour as needed

oil as needed

1 onion, small dice

1 carrot, small dice

1 celery stalk, small dice

1 garlic clove, small dice

1 ounce tomato paste

1 ounce flour

6 ounces red wine

2 cups beef stock

2 sprigs thyme

salt and pepper to taste

Preheat a pot with oil, dust ribs with flour, sear, and set aside.

Caramelize the vegetables in the pot, add tomato paste, then flour.

Deglaze with wine and stock, stirring well. Simmer.

Add ribs, cover, and braise in a 375-degree oven until tender.

Strain the sauce, season, and combine with ribs.

Serving Suggestions:
Pairs well with polenta, savoyard potatoes, or risotto.

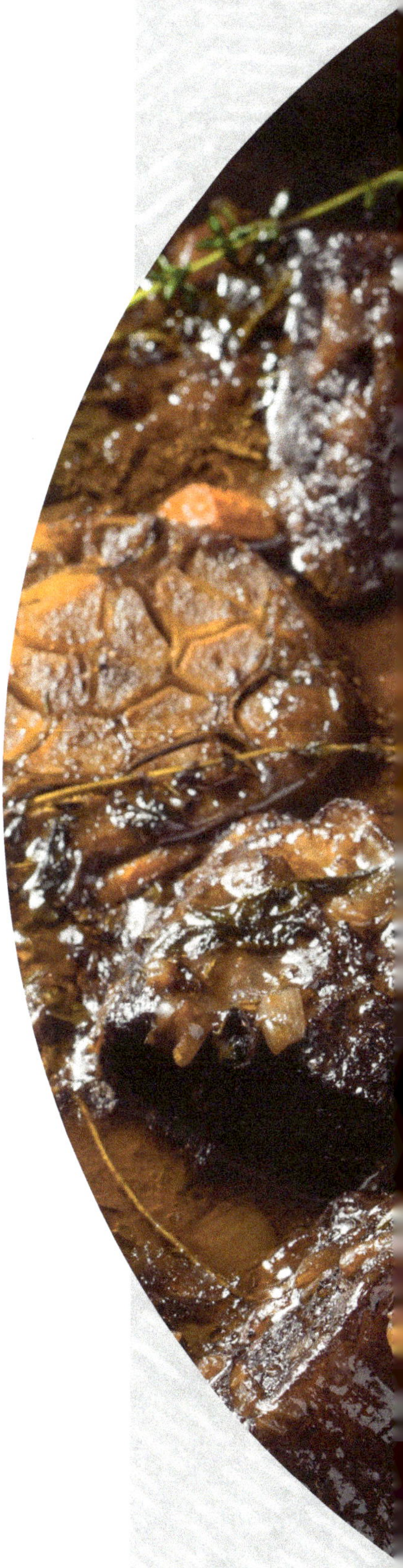

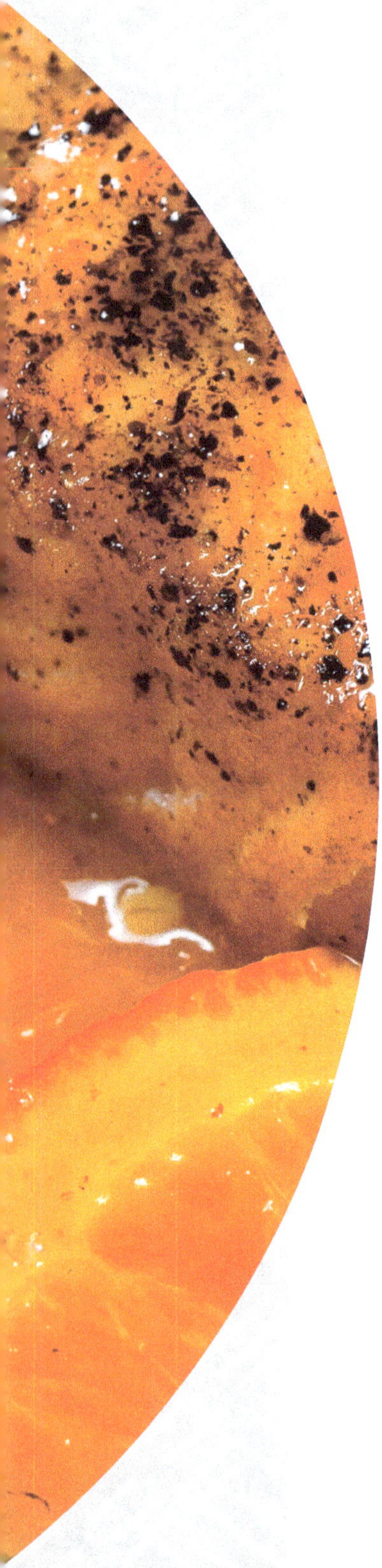

SALMON WITH ORANGE GLAZE

16 ounces salmon fillets, boneless and skinless

4 ounces ginger root, peeled and chopped

1 tablespoon Sichuan peppercorns

2 ounces fresh orange juice

¼ cup granulated sugar

2 tablespoons black pepper

1 tablespoon peanut oil

2 tablespoons soy sauce

2 tablespoons orange concentrate

½ bunch cilantro

1 stick lemongrass

Combine ginger, orange juice, peppercorns, cilantro, and lemongrass in a food processor and chop finely.

Roll the salmon in the mixture. Allow to marinate at room temperature for up to 2 hours.

In a separate bowl, mix sugar and black pepper. Heat peanut oil over medium-high heat.

Press the presentation side of the salmon into the sugar mixture.

Sauté the presentation side for 2-3 minutes. Ensure sugar doesn't brown.

Add soy sauce and orange concentrate, swirling to deglaze the pan.

Turn salmon to the presentation side up and let it finish cooking.

Serving Suggestions:
Serve the salmon with summer squash noodles and optional jasmine rice for an Asian-inspired meal.

FRENCH TOAST WITH SPICED SYRUP

Spiced Syrup:

1 cup water

1 cup packed brown sugar

1 cinnamon stick

1 star anise

1 teaspoon orange zest

2 tablespoons whipping cream

¼ teaspoon clove

French Toast:

1 loaf good quality bread

6 large eggs

¾ cup whipping cream

¾ cup whole milk

¼ cup sugar

2 tablespoons unsalted butter

¼ teaspoon vanilla

½ teaspoon cinnamon

¼ teaspoon nutmeg

For the syrup, combine water, brown sugar, and spices in a medium saucepan. Bring to a boil and let boil for 5-7 minutes.

Reduce to a simmer for 10 minutes and then set aside.

For the French toast, combine eggs, milk, cream, and flavorings in a large bowl. Set aside.

Preheat griddle to 350 degrees or heat a large sauté pan on medium-high heat. Dip bread slices into the mixture for about a minute per slice. Drain excess and cook on griddle for about 2 minutes per side or until golden brown.

Serve immediately.

CILANTRO VINAIGRETTE

2 tablespoons cilantro, leaves only

½ cup fresh orange juice

½ tablespoon rice wine vinegar

½ tablespoon lime juice

¼ cup honey

1 clove garlic

1 teaspoon ginger root, peeled and minced

2 ounces olive oil

salt and pepper to taste

Combine all ingredients in a blender and purée until smooth.

CARROT-GINGER SOUP

2 cloves garlic, peeled and chopped

2 tablespoons vegetable oil

½ cup yellow onions, diced

3 cups carrots, diced, peeled, and minced

2 tablespoons ginger root, peeled

2 cups sweet potatoes, peeled

3 cups vegetable or chicken stock

1 tablespoon fresh lemon juice

1 tablespoon honey

½ cup coconut milk

1 bay leaf

salt and pepper to taste

2 tablespoons cilantro, chopped

Heat the oil, add onions, and sauté for 5 minutes until translucent.

Add bay leaf, garlic, and ginger and sauté for 3 more minutes.

Add carrots, potatoes, stock, salt, and pepper. Bring to a boil, then simmer until vegetables are tender (around 25 minutes).

Once tender, purée the mixture until smooth. Reheat on low.

Add lemon juice, honey, and coconut milk. Stir thoroughly. Adjust thickness with additional stock if needed.

Garnish with chopped cilantro when serving.

KALUA PIG SPRING ROLLS WITH PINEAPPLE DIPPING SAUCE

6 ounces Kalua Pig, prepared

1 tablespoon vegetable oil

¼ cup red onion, small dice

2 cloves garlic, minced

¾ cup water chestnuts, medium dice

2 cups Napa cabbage, shredded

½ cup red cabbage, shredded

¼ cup green onion, chopped

1 tablespoon carrot, grated

1 tablespoon oyster sauce

salt and pepper to taste

10 spring roll wrappers

1 egg, beaten with 1 teaspoon water

vegetable oil for frying

Preheat oven to 400 degrees.

Score the pork on all sides with 0.25-inch deep slits about 1-inch apart.

Combine the salt, liquid smoke, and garlic. Rub the liquid smoke mixture all around the pork butt.

Wrap the pork butt in banana leaves and tie with string to hold in place.

Place in an appropriate pan and cover tightly with a lid or foil.

Bake in the preheated oven for 1 hour. Lower the temperature to 350 degrees and cook for 2 hours until tender.

Remove from the pan. Let it cool slightly and then shred the meat.

SAUTÉED TOMATOES

½ ounce butter, unsalted

2 ounces onion, chopped

1 ounce green bell pepper, chopped

18 ounces tomatoes, peeled, seeded, and quartered

salt and pepper to taste

Melt the butter in a sauté pan.

Add the onions and bell peppers and sauté until onions are translucent.

Add the tomatoes and cook until thoroughly heated.

Season to taste.

CELERIAC PURÉE

2 large celeriac (celery root), peeled and cubed

2 cloves garlic, mashed

1 bay leaf

½ cup cream

¼ teaspoon fresh grated nutmeg

kosher salt and pepper to taste

Bring a large pot of water to a boil.

Once boiling, add a pinch of salt to the water.

Add the celeriac and boil until tender.

Once tender, drain and remove the bay leaf. Add 3 tablespoons unsalted butter, and mash.

Stir in the cream and adjust seasoning.

Serve warm.

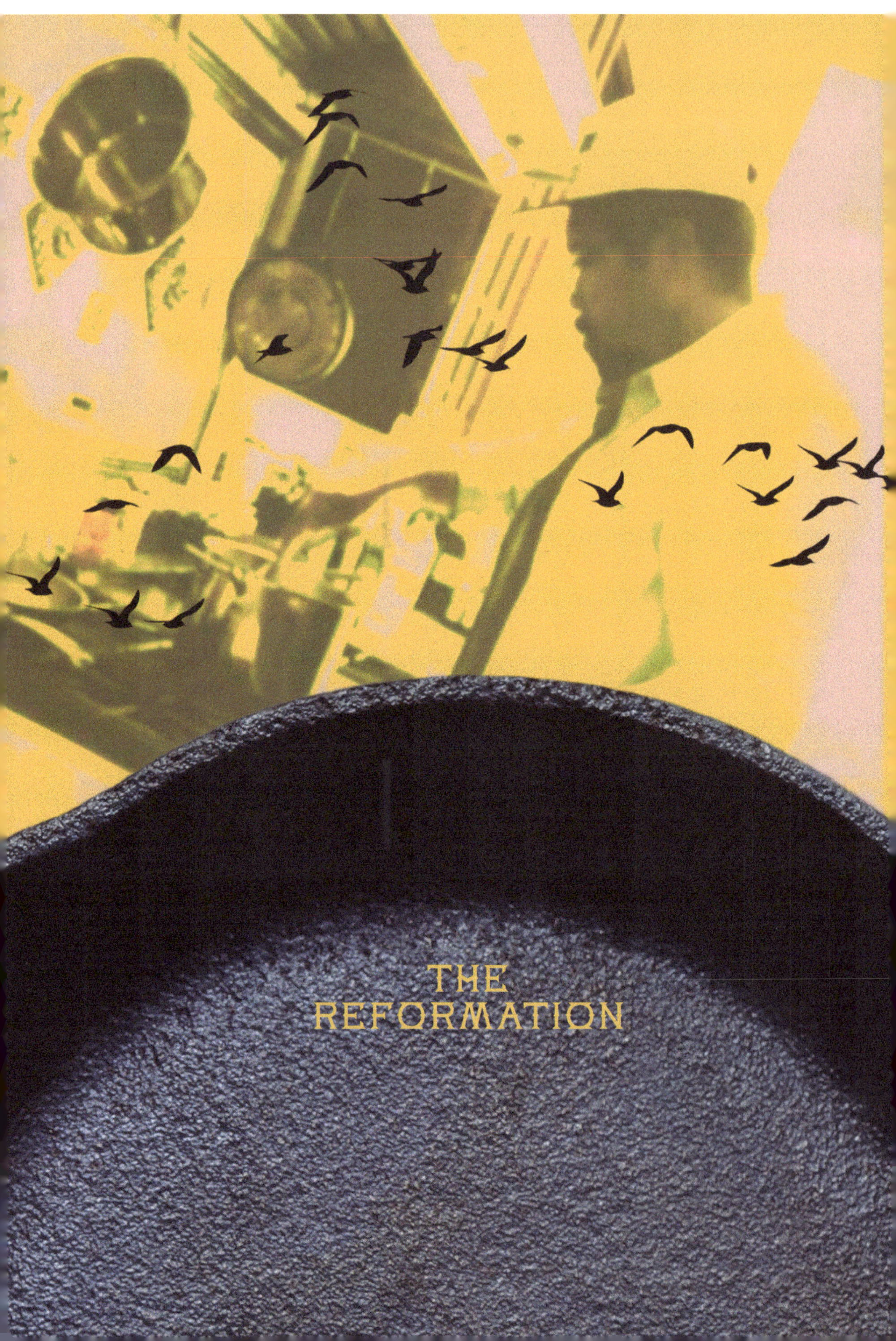
THE
REFORMATION

We all have those phases in life when we're trying to carve our identities, often pushing away from the known to explore the unknown. The rebellious stage, as I fondly refer to it. The sheer act of defying the norms, breaking the status quo, or simply wanting to be different, can sometimes pull us in directions we hadn't anticipated.

I too went through such a phase, but emerged unscathed and unharmed. The wake-up call for me was a profound loss. My grandmother, Clara Goodman, the keystone of my culinary world, passed away. The chasm left by her absence made me realize that in my quest to be different, I had lost a piece of myself. I was so wrapped up in standing out that I overlooked the essence of who I was.

With the weight of that realization, my culinary journey took a turn. I had an epiphany. Being a chef, much like being a person, wasn't about fitting into a mold or ticking off boxes. I didn't need to restrict myself or try to fit a predetermined label. It was about passion, memories, and most importantly, authenticity.

In a world that is constantly evolving, going back can be as revolutionary as forging ahead. There wasn't any rule book that prohibited revisiting the past, so I decided to go on a culinary pilgrimage. I dusted off old recipes, those that had ignited my passion for food, and started cooking. It was like meeting an old friend after years – familiar, yet different.

Rediscovering those flavors was more than just about food. It was a journey of self-reclamation. Every dish was a memory, a piece of advice, a story that my grandmother once shared. I realized then, that sometimes, to move forward, you need to take a step back.

Today, as I stand in my kitchen, I know I am a blend of the past and the present. I honor the traditional while embracing the contemporary. My cooking, much like me, has come full circle. I have found my flavors, and in them, I have found myself.

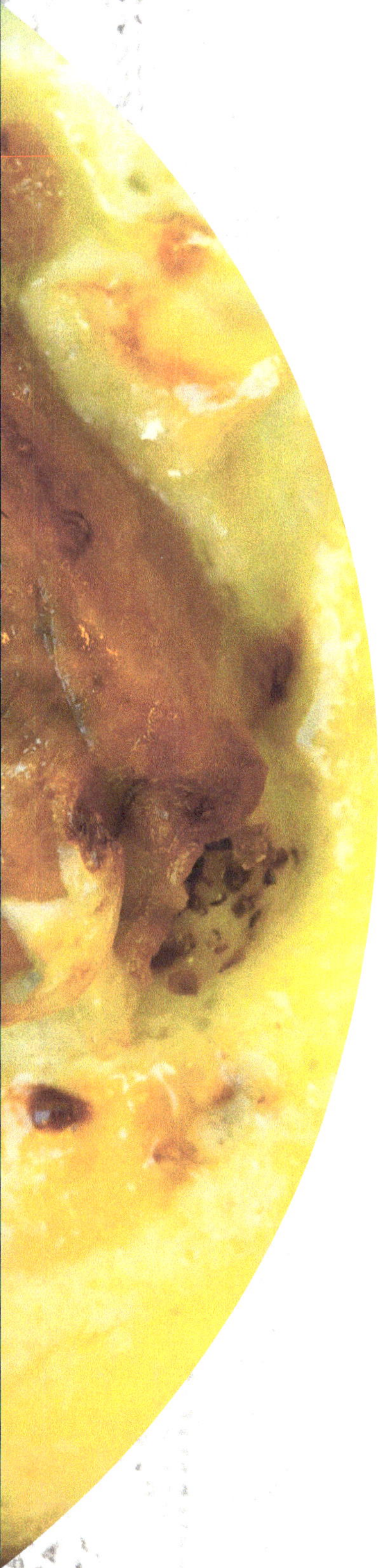

SAVOYARD POTATOES

2 pounds potatoes

1 ounce clarified butter

2 ounces diced onion

2 ounces pancetta or bacon

chicken stock as needed

salt and pepper, to taste

Peel and wash the potatoes. Slice them ¼ inch thick, keeping the slices together. Do not wash after slicing.

In a sauté pan, heat the clarified butter, then add onions and bacon. Sweat over medium heat.

Deglaze the pan with chicken stock.

Add the potatoes to the pan and cover with more stock. Place the pan over medium heat, bringing it to a simmer.

Transfer to a 375-degree oven and bake until potatoes are tender and most of the stock has evaporated.

STUFFED TOMATOES

4 Roma tomatoes, peeled and seeded

2 ounces clarified butter

1 ounces finely diced onions

12 ounces finely chopped mushrooms

1 tablespoon finely chopped parsley

salt and pepper, to taste

In a sauté pan, melt the clarified butter. Add onions and sweat until translucent.

Add the mushrooms and cook until their released liquid evaporates. Season as desired.

Cut the tops off the peeled Roma tomatoes and remove seeds.

Season the inside with salt and pepper.

Stuff each tomato with the duxelles mixture.

Bake in a 375-degree oven until hot.

RISOTTO

1 ounce clarified butter

2 ounces onion, finely diced

1 cup Arborio rice

3 cups chicken stock

½ cup dry white wine

1 ounce Parmesan cheese

1 ounce unsalted butter

salt and pepper, to taste

In a saucepot, melt butter. Add onions and sweat them, followed by the rice, stirring until well-coated without browning.

Add the chicken stock and seasoning, then bring to a simmer, and simmer stirring occasionally for about 18-20 minutes.

Add white wine, Parmesan cheese, and whole butter. Stir well.

Serve immediately.

Tip: To customize your risotto, add saffron, pesto, asparagus, peas, or other ingredients as suggested.

RATATOUILLE

½ ounce olive oil

¼ ounce minced garlic

2 ounces small diced onion

½ ounce tomato paste

6 ounces chicken stock

2 ounces yellow squash (¼-inch dice)

4 ounces zucchini (¼-inch dice)

1 ounces green pepper (¼-inch dice)

3 ounces eggplant (¼-inch dice)

6 ounces mushrooms (¼-inch dice)

3 ounces tomato (¼-inch dice, peeled)

salt and pepper, to taste

1 tablespoon chopped basil

In a pan, sauté garlic and onion in oil until translucent. Add tomato paste and pincé.

Deglaze with chicken stock, then add all vegetables.

Stew the mixture until the liquid almost fully evaporates and the vegetables are tender.

Season and garnish with chopped basil.

Tip: To pincé means to cook the tomato paste with garlic and onion until it forms a thick paste.

CAULIFLOWER AU GRATIN

1 head of cauliflower

1 cup Béchamel sauce

1 ounce Parmesan cheese

1 ounce butter

Prepare cauliflower and simmer in salted water until tender.

Drain, chill, and then coat the cauliflower with Béchamel sauce.

Sprinkle with Parmesan cheese and place a dab of butter on top.

Reheat in a 350-degree oven until hot.

SHRIMP WITH VODKA SAUCE

3 pounds shrimp, peeled and deveined

3 tablespoons olive oil

1 cup vodka

2 cups seafood stock

¼ cup fresh lemon juice

2 cups tomatoes, chopped

2 cloves garlic

3 tablespoons fresh chopped basil

1 cup heavy cream

In a saucepan, reduce stock, lemon juice, and heavy cream by half.

In a sauté pan, heat olive oil and garlic. Sear the shrimp then pour off fat.

Add tomatoes and deglaze with vodka.

Add the reduced sauce and cook shrimp until done.

Serve over bowtie pasta.

SCALLOPINI "MILANESE"

8 scallopini, prepared

salt and pepper, to taste

standard breading procedure, as needed

clarified butter as needed

Prepare the scallopini and season with salt and pepper.

Apply standard breading procedure to the scallopini.

Heat sauté pan with butter and pan-fry the scallopini until golden brown on both sides.

Remove from heat, drain on a paper towel. Serve immediately.

SCALLOPINI "PICCATA"

8 scallopini, prepared

salt and pepper to taste

flour as needed

eggs, whipped

Parmesan cheese, grated

clarified butter as needed

Prepare the scallopini and season.

Dip in flour on both sides, shake off excess.

Place the scallops in the egg and cheese mixture. Sear on a pan with clarified butter, draining the excess egg wash.

Pan-fry on both sides until golden brown, remove from heat and serve immediately.

CHICAGO DEEP DISH PIZZA DOUGH

5 ounces milk

1 ½ ounces butter

1 tablespoon dry yeast

2 ounces water at 110°F

1 tablespoon sugar

½ teaspoon salt

1 ounce cornmeal

2 eggs, beaten

10 ounces all-purpose flour

Scald the milk, remove from heat, add the butter, and cool to 125 degrees.

Combine water, yeast, and sugar; let it stand for 10 minutes.

Pour milk into the yeast mixture, add salt, cornmeal, eggs, and ²/₃ of the flour into a large bowl. Stir until smooth, then add the remaining flour to create a sticky dough.

Place on a floured surface and knead for 10 minutes. Place in a greased bowl, cover with plastic wrap, and let it rise until doubled, about 1 ½-2 hours.

Punch down the dough and let it rise again until doubled, about 30 minutes.

CHICAGO DEEP DISH PIZZA

1 ounce butter

4 ounces onion, diced

1 clove garlic, minced

2 ounces tomato, diced

2 ounces tomato purée

1 pinch dry basil

1 pinch dry oregano

salt and pepper to taste

1 recipe Chicago deep dish pizza dough

8 ounces Italian sausage, sliced

12 ounces mozzarella, grated

1 ounce Parmesan cheese, grated

For the tomato sauce: Sweat the onions and garlic in butter, stir in the diced tomato, tomato purée, basil, oregano, salt, and pepper to taste; simmer for 30 minutes until thick.

For the pizza: Preheat oven to 400 degrees.

Divide the dough in half. Grease 2 x 9-inch round cake pans, roll dough into 9-inch circles. Line the pans with the dough, pressing it so it goes halfway up the sides.

Sauté the sausage, let it cool, then slice into ½-inch thick slices.

Line dough with 3 ounces of grated mozzarella, cover with sauce, arrange half of the sausage, then cover with another 3 ounces of mozzarella and Parmesan.

Bake in the oven until golden brown, approximately 25 minutes.

FIELD GREENS WITH MUSHROOMS

4 ounces Mesclun Salad Mix, cleaned

12 tomato leaves, prepared

½ pint mushrooms, sliced

Fried onions as needed

Dressing:

1 ounce sherry vinegar

2 ounces olive oil

2 ounces chicken stock

2 hard boiled egg yolks, finely chopped

salt and white pepper to taste

Prepare all the ingredients as listed.

Marinate the tomato leaves and mushrooms in the vinaigrette.

At serving time, remove the tomato leaves, add the salad mix and toss.

Plate 3 tomato leaves, then top with the mushroom and tossed mesclun salad mix. Garnish with fried onions.

TOMATO-CHILI WATER VINAIGRETTE

4 ounces tomato purée

2 ounces chili water

1 ounce olive oil

For Chili Water:

2 cups water

1 teaspoon salt

1 teaspoon rice wine vinegar

1 garlic clove, crushed

6 dried Thai chili peppers, red

Blend the tomato purée, chili water, and oil to emulsify.

Sterilize a 16-ounce bottle by boiling in water for a few minutes, then let it cool. Place salt, vinegar, garlic, and chili peppers into the bottle.

Bring the water to a boil and pour into the bottle. Stir with a chopstick and leave for three days under refrigeration to mature.

HONEY PEPPERED SALMON

1 ¼ cups olive oil

⅓ cup honey

5/8 cup Dijon mustard

15 garlic cloves, minced

3 ⅓ tablespoons cayenne

2 ½ teaspoons ground coriander

5/8 cup lemon juice

salt and pepper to taste

10 6-ounce salmon steaks or fillets

Combine the olive oil, honey, mustard, garlic, cayenne, coriander, lemon juice, salt, and pepper in a shallow dish. Mix well.

Add the salmon and marinate for 30 minutes.

Place the salmon in a greased baking dish.

Bake at 350 degrees for 6-7 minutes per side.

Garnish with dill sprigs.

SPAETZLE

8 ounces all-purpose flour

2 eggs

5 ounces water

salt and pepper to taste

oil as needed

clarified butter as needed

In a mixing bowl, place the flour and create a well in the center. Crack the eggs into this well.

Slowly add the water to the bowl while mixing, then incorporate the seasoning. Mix until a medium stiff paste forms, using your hands if necessary.

In a large saucepot, bring salted water to a gentle simmer. Add a dash of oil to the simmering water.

Press the dough through a colander into the simmering water. Do this until spaetzle pieces start to float to the surface.

Using a skimmer, remove the floating spaetzle and immediately transfer them to a bowl of cold water to halt the cooking process. Once cooled, drain the spaetzle thoroughly.

In a pan, heat some clarified butter over medium heat. Sauté the spaetzle until lightly browned, seasoning with salt and pepper according to taste.

PROVENCAL SWEET POTATOES

16 ounces sweet potatoes, peeled and cubed

2 tablespoons honey

3 tablespoons butter

1 ounce red onion, diced

1 bay leaf

1 ½ teaspoons herbs des Provence

1 teaspoon orange zest

2 cloves garlic, minced

8 ounces vegetable stock

salt and pepper to taste

Heat a heavy sauce pot to medium heat.

Sauté in butter, garlic, red onion, and bay leaf, about 2 minutes.

Add sweet potatoes and sauté for 5 minutes.

Add vegetable stock, cover with a lid, and cook until tender. Stir occasionally.

At the end add honey, orange zest, and herbs de Provence.

Serve immediately or at room temperature.

CREAM OF MUSHROOM SOUP

3 ounces clarified butter

4 ounces onion, diced

2 ounces celery, diced

2 ounces leeks, diced

2 pounds mushrooms, diced

3 ounces all-purpose flour

1 ½ quarts cold chicken stock

1 cup heavy cream, heated

salt and pepper to taste

Sweat onion, celery, and mushrooms in butter.

Add flour and stir until absorbed, then add chicken stock. Stir to dissolve the roux and bring to a simmer.

Turn down the heat and simmer for 30 minutes.

Purée the soup in a blender. Bring back to a simmer, season with salt and pepper.

Add the cream to the soup.

Serve with a garnish of sliced sautéed mushrooms and chopped parsley.

ESPAGNOLE (BROWN) SAUCE

3 ounces oil

8 ounces mirepoix, prepared

2 ounces tomato paste

5 ounces all-purpose flour

4 quarts veal stock

Heat the oil, add the mirepoix, and caramelize.

Add tomato paste and cook out [pincé].

Add flour and stir until absorbed by oil.

Add brown stock and bring to a simmer.

Continue to simmer until sauce has reduced by half. Approximately 2 quarts.

Strain through double cheesecloth.

Tip: Mirepoix is a mix of carrot, celery, and onion.

BÉCHAMEL SAUCE

4 ounces oil

2 ounces onion, diced

4 ounces all-purpose flour

2 quarts whole milk

salt and white pepper to taste

Heat the oil in a stainless steel saucepot. Sweat the onions and add flour to make white roux.

Add half the milk and stir vigorously until thickened. Add the remaining milk and repeat.

Reduce the heat to low and simmer for 30 minutes. Adjust seasoning.

Strain through a double cheesecloth.

MAYONNAISE

2 egg yolks

¼ teaspoon dry mustard

¼ ounce lemon juice

1 ½ cups vegetable oil

½ ounce cider vinegar

½ ounce water

salt and white pepper to taste

¼ ounce lemon juice to taste

Combine egg yolks, dry mustard, and lemon juice in a bowl. Mix with a soft balloon whip.

Very slowly add oil, constantly beating until an emulsion has occurred (the oil is incorporated and the mayonnaise is thick).

Adjust the flavor and thickness with vinegar and water.

Adjust the seasoning with salt, white pepper, and additional lemon juice.

RISSOLÉE POTATOES

2 pounds
Russet potatoes,
¾-inch diced

clarified butter
as needed

salt and pepper
to taste

Peel and wash potatoes, ensuring no eyes remain, and place them in cold water.

Trim and shape into ¾-inch cubes.

Parboil for 2 minutes. Drain, cool, and pat dry before using.
Pan fry in clarified butter until tender and golden brown.

Season with salt and pepper to taste while hot.

PANÉED CHICKEN

Seasoning mixture:

3 ounces ketchup

2 ½ ounces Creole mustard

1 ½ tablespoons white pepper

1 ½ tablespoons cayenne pepper

5 tablespoons paprika

¾ teaspoon thyme (dried or fresh)

⅓ teaspoon sage (dried or fresh)

⅓ teaspoon basil (dried or fresh)

Breading:

7 large eggs

3 tablespoons vegetable oil

5 ounces breadcrumbs

2 ½ pounds chicken breast, deboned and flat

1 ½ tablespoons kosher salt

vegetable oil as needed

Combine the ingredients of the seasoning mix in a small bowl and mix thoroughly.

Combine the eggs and 3 tablespoons of vegetable oil in a pan. Beat well.

Combine 2 tablespoons of the seasoning mix with the breadcrumbs and blend in a food processor. Set aside.

Spread an even layer of the seasoning mix over both sides of the chicken, then soak the chicken in the egg mixture for 15-30 minutes.

In a large skillet, heat about ¼-inch vegetable oil to at least 300 degrees.

Remove the chicken from the egg mixture, drain excess batter, and coat with breadcrumbs. Shake off excess and gently place in hot oil. Pan-fry until golden brown and reaches an internal temperature of 165 degrees.

Drain on paper towels and serve immediately.

MORNAY SAUCE

1 tablespoon unsalted butter

1 tablespoon all-purpose flour

¼ teaspoon salt

¼ teaspoon nutmeg

¼ teaspoon red pepper

½ cup chicken stock

½ cup half & half

½ cup shredded cheddar

Melt butter in small saucepan. Blend in flour, salt, nutmeg, and red pepper.

Cook over low heat, stirring constantly until smooth and bubbly.

Immediately stir in chicken stock and half & half.

Heat to boiling, stirring constantly.

Boil and stir for 1 minute.

Stir in cheese until melted.

CRAB CAKES

3 tablespoons unsalted butter

1 tablespoon chopped green onion

2 tablespoons small diced red bell pepper

1 clove garlic, minced

3 tablespoons Dijon mustard

1 egg

½ teaspoon red pepper

½ cup grated Parmesan cheese

1 pound lump crabmeat

2 teaspoons olive oil

Melt butter and sauté onion, bell pepper, and garlic, then set aside and let cool.

In a bowl, combine cream, egg, pepper, ½ cup breadcrumbs, sautéed veggies, mustard, salt, and pepper, and crabmeat just to combine.

Mix remaining breadcrumbs and Parmesan cheese.

Form the crab cakes then dredge in breadcrumb mixture and pan fry.

CREAM OF POBLANO SOUP

12 poblano peppers, roasted, peeled, and seeded

2 jalapenos, roasted, peeled, and seeded

2 cloves of roasted garlic

3 onions, chopped

16 ounces vegetable stock

8 ounces heavy cream

Kosher salt and black pepper, to taste

Roast the vegetables at 350 degrees for 15 minutes.

Once roasted, let rest for 5 minutes in a Ziploc bag.

Remove from bag, peel, and deseed. Cook in stock for 5 minutes.

Remove half of the stock, puree the soup. Once puréed, add the cream. If too thick, add the reserved stock.

Adjust seasoning and serve.

CHILLED ASPARAGUS SOUP

14 ounces chopped asparagus

2 ounces cleaned and chopped leeks

1 chopped clove of garlic

½ ounce chopped rosemary

½ ounce chopped thyme

½ ounce chopped oregano

½ ounce chopped chervil (optional)

1 gallon water

Kosher salt and black pepper, to taste

Take all chopped ingredients, place them into a pot, and cover with water and bring to a boil.

Once it has come to a boil, check asparagus for tenderness.

If tender, remove 8 ounces of liquid and reserve.

Purée the soup, if it's too thick then add some of reserve liquid and chill until ready to serve.

Serving Suggestions: Serve with a dollop of crème fraiche and some chopped tarragon.

SAMBAL

10 hot peppers (like 10 Thai chili pepper or 20 serrano peppers)

2 tablespoons dried shrimp paste

¾ teaspoon salt

Wash peppers and discard stems. Allow to air-dry or use paper towels to dry off.

Roughly cut up the pepper and place into a blender with all of the ingredients.

Process until all the peppers are chopped into fine pieces, almost a purée.

Spoon into a clean container and keep refrigerated.

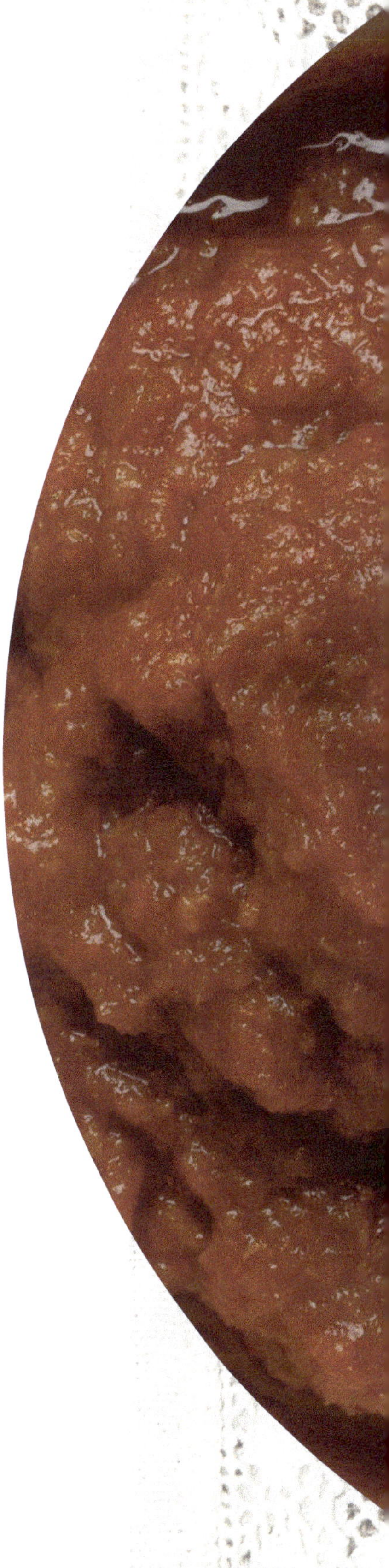

LEMON BUTTER SAUCE

2 ounces butter

½ ounce fresh squeezed lemon juice

½ ounce dry white wine

2 ounces cold and cubed butter

chopped parsley

Heat saucepan, add butter and heat to a light noisette (light brown).

Deglaze with lemon juice and white wine.

Bring to a simmer, season to taste, and remove from heat.

Stir in the cold butter to monté the sauce. Do not apply any more heat after adding cold butter.

Add chopped parsley.

Note: Make in small batches as needed only. Will not stay emulsified at high or low temperatures.

SEAFOOD CRÊPES

Crêpes:

1 cup all-purpose flour

½ cup whole milk

3 large eggs

2 tablespoons butter

¼ teaspoon black pepper

¼ teaspoon salt

Filling:

1 twelve-ounce container plump crabmeat, picked

12 ounces shrimp, cooked, chopped, and cooled

12 ounces lobster, cooked, chopped, cooled

8 ounces ricotta

8 ounces fontina

1 small container mascarpone

2 each garlic, grated

1/8 teaspoon fresh grated nutmeg

¼ teaspoon paprika

¼ bunch parsley, chopped

salt and pepper to taste

Mix batter and let sit for 1 hour.

Heat a crêpe pan or a non-stick skillet over moderate heat until hot.

Grease the pan lightly with melted butter.

Stir the batter.

Fill a ¼ cup measuring cup with batter and pour into the pan.

Tilt and rotate the pan quickly to cover the bottom. Return excess batter to the bowl.

Loosen the edge of the crêpe with a spatula and cook for 1 minute, flip and lightly cook the other side.

Transfer to plate.

BASIL VINAIGRETTE

8 tablespoons olive oil

½ teaspoon fennel reed, toasted

1 bunch fresh basil

1 clove garlic

¼ teaspoon salt

1/8 teaspoon pepper

2 tablespoons lemon juice

CURRY SAUCE

1 tablespoon cornstarch

⅓ cup unsweetened coconut milk

2 tablespoons corn oil

1 small onion or shallot, minced

1 teaspoon ginger root, peeled and grated

1 tablespoon curry powder

1 dash Tabasco sauce

2 cups chicken stock

1 teaspoon Kosher salt

ROASTED GARLIC PESTO SAUCE

1 ¼ cups
extra virgin olive oil

½ cup pine nuts,
toasted

1 bulb garlic, roasted

2 ½ teaspoons
sea salt

2 ½ bunches fresh basil
leaves, torn

1 ¼ cups Parmesan
cheese, fresh grated

BASIL SOY SAUCE

1 cup
Balsamic vinegar

½ cup
soy sauce

BUTTERNUT SQUASH AND PUMPKIN GINGER SOUP

16 ounces butternut squash, peeled, seeded, and cubed

16 ounces pumpkin, peeled, seeded, and cubed

1 tablespoon vegetable oil

2 tablespoons ginger root, minced

1 ½ cups sweet onions, small dice

1 cup carrots, small dice

1 cup celery, small dice
½ cup white wine (optional)

2 cups chicken stock

½ teaspoon fennel seeds, whole

1 teaspoon cumin seeds, whole

½ teaspoon dried chili flakes

1 teaspoon turmeric

1 each bay leaf

1 each star anise

2 tablespoons basil, fresh chopped

1 teaspoon Kosher salt

2 slices ginger root

1 each Keffir lime leaf or regular lime leaf

1 cup heavy cream

2 ounces Enoki mushrooms

2 tablespoons parsley, chopped

ASIAN DRESSING

¼ cup soy sauce

1 ounce white wine vinegar

1 ounce vegetable oil

3 ounces sake

3 ounces shallot, minced

1 tablespoon passion fruit concentrate or fresh

½ tablespoon ginger root, grated

¼ teaspoon sesame oil

PLUM DRESSING

2 ounces plum sauce

3 tablespoons lime juice, fresh

3 tablespoons rice wine vinegar

3 tablespoons spicy fish sauce

1 ounce granulated sugar

1 tablespoon sesame oil

SPICY FISH SAUCE

4 tablespoons red wine vinegar

2 tablespoons water

¼ cup granulated sugar

4 tablespoons fish sauce, Thailand

1 Thai chili pepper, minced

CHAR SIU

2 pounds pork butt, cut into 5x3x2" pieces

1 tablespoon Hawaiian sea salt or Kosher salt

Marinade:

¼ cup soy sauce

2 tablespoons dry sherry wine

1 ounce granulated sugar

1 tablespoon Chinese five spice powder

1 teaspoon ginger root, sliced and crushed

Preheat oven to 350 degrees.

Rub the pork with salt and refrigerate for 1 hour.

Combine the marinade ingredients, Heat them in a saucepan for 1 minute to dissolve the sugar. Cool.

Marinate the pork in the refrigerator for 24 hours or at room temperature for 2 hours. Reserve the marinade.

Place meat on a rack over ¼" of water in a shallow roasting pan.

Roast in a preheated oven for 30 minutes. Turn over, reduce heat and continue roasting for 1 hour at 325 degrees, brushing occasionally with the reserved marinade.

Remove from oven and let rest for 10 minutes.

Cut into thin, bite-size slices that can be eaten with chopsticks. Serve hot or cold.

DEEP-FRIED CALAMARI SALAD

2 cups all-purpose flour

2 tablespoons paprika

1 pound calamari, cleaned and cut into rings

Kosher salt and black pepper to taste

olive oil for deep-frying as needed

4 cups mesclun salad greens

½ cup red bell pepper, julienne

½ cup yellow bell pepper, julienne

½ cup sweet onion, julienne

½ cup sautéed, sliced cremini mushrooms

1 ½ cups cucumber, peeled, seeded, sliced

¾ cup tomatoes, seeded and cut into wedges

basil vinaigrette

Heat oil to 350 degrees.

Combine flour and paprika.

Season the calamari with Kosher salt and pepper.

Toss the calamari in the flour mixture. Dust off the excess flour.

Deep-fry until golden brown.

Toss salad greens with basil vinaigrette.

Arrange salad greens and vegetables on cold plates. Place calamari on top. Serve additional dressing on the side.

SEARED SALMON WITH AVOCADO, SHRIMP, AND MANGO SALSA

Salmon:

cooking spray

4 (6 ounce) salmon fillets (about 1 inch thick)

¼ teaspoon salt

¼ teaspoon black pepper

Salsa:

1 cup cubed, peeled ripe mango

½ cup medium shrimp, cooked and peeled

¼ cup chopped red onion

2 tablespoons chopped fresh cilantro

2 tablespoons fresh lime juice

1 tablespoon olive oil

1 jalapeño pepper, seeded and chopped

6 cups gourmet salad greens

2 tablespoons fresh lime juice

¼ teaspoon salt

1/8 teaspoon freshly ground black pepper

1 peeled avocado, cut into ¼-inch wedges

To prepare salmon, heat a large nonstick skillet coated with cooking spray over medium heat. Sprinkle fish with ¼ teaspoon salt and ¼ teaspoon black pepper. Add fish to pan, and cook for 9 minutes or until the fish flakes easily when it is tested with a fork, turning once.

To prepare salsa, combine mango and the next 6 ingredients (mango through jalapeño) in a medium bowl, and toss well to combine.

Combine the salad greens, juice, ¼ teaspoon salt, 1/8 teaspoon black pepper, and avocado wedges in a large bowl; toss gently to combine. Arrange a salmon fillet on each of 4 plates; top each with ½ cup salsa and 1 ½ cups salad mixture.

BEEF SATÉ WITH PEANUT DIPPING SAUCE

1 (3 ½ ounce) bag boil-in-bag long-grain rice

1 (1 pound) flank steak, trimmed

2 tablespoons Hoisin sauce

¼ teaspoon salt

cooking spray

3 tablespoons chopped fresh cilantro

2 tablespoons light coconut milk

1 tablespoon low-sodium soy sauce

1 ½ tablespoons creamy peanut butter

1 teaspoon sugar

1 teaspoon fresh lime juice

½ teaspoon red curry paste

Preheat broiler.

Cook rice according to package directions, omitting salt and fat. Drain; cover and keep warm.

Cut steak diagonally across grain into ¼-inch thick slices. Combine steak and hoisin in a bowl; toss to coat.

Thread steak onto each of 8 (8 inch) skewers; sprinkle evenly with salt.

Place skewers on a broiler pan coated with cooking spray; broil 3 minutes on each side or until desired degree of doneness.

Sprinkle skewers with cilantro.

Combine coconut milk and remaining ingredients in a bowl, stirring until smooth.

Serve with skewers and rice.

ROASTED PORK LOIN WITH GARLIC MASHED POTATOES

16 ounces pork loin

6 ounces Dijon mustard

16 ounces potatoes, peeled, quartered

1 clove garlic, finely minced

8 ounces sweet butter, melted

10 ounces heavy cream

kosher salt and black pepper to taste

Season the pork loin with salt and pepper and smear Dijon mustard on the top and bake at 375 degrees for 20 minutes.

In a pot, boil potatoes until fork tender, drain and dry. Once dry run through a ricer.

Once it has been riced, add butter, cream, garlic, and salt and pepper.

Take out pork loin and let rest for 10 minutes.

Once rested, slice on a bias.

Fan the pork loin on a plate by the mashed potatoes.

Pour the natural juices over it.

GARLIC OPAKAPAKA WITH PINEAPPLE COCONUT RICE

1 Opakapaka fish, fillet

1 pineapple, peeled, cored, chunked

14 ounces coconut milk

6 ounces long grain rice

kosher salt and black pepper to taste

3 ounces coconut flakes, toasted

Season the fish fillet with salt and pepper and grill.

In a saucepot, combine rice, coconut milk, and pineapple and bring to a boil.

Serve on a rectangle plate with the fillet on top of the rice and garnish with toasted coconut.

Substitutions:
If you cannot find opakapaka, you can substitute halibut, cod, swordfish, or any firm white fish.

GARLIC HERB CHICKEN WITH MUSHROOM RISOTTO

2 chicken breast, washed

5 cloves garlic, minced

0.5 ounce tarragon, finely minced

0.5 ounce rosemary, finely minced

0.5 ounces oregano, finely minced

0.5 ounces thyme, finely minced

12 ounces wild mushrooms, cleaned, roughly chopped

1 ounce sweet butter

2.5 ounces olive oil

12 ounces Arborio rice

2 ounces white wine

1 quart chicken stock

kosher salt and black pepper to taste

1 each shallot, minced

Preheat oven to 375 degrees.

Season the chicken breasts and place on a sheet pan.

Cook in the oven for 10 minutes.

In a saucepot, heat butter, olive oil, shallots, mushrooms, and Arborio rice, stirring until coated.

Deglaze with white wine.

Continue cooking, slowly adding liquid until the mixture reaches a creamy consistency and the rice is fully cooked.

Serve on a circular plate and garnish with a sprig of thyme.

SPICE RUBBED FILET MIGNON WITH CREAMED SPINACH

8 ounces filet mignon

0.5 ounces coriander

0.5 ounces lavender

0.5 ounces salt

0.25 ounces cracked black pepper

0.5 ounces cardamom

11 ounces baby spinach

10 ounces heavy cream

kosher salt and black pepper to taste

2 ounces olive oil

Roll the filet mignon in the spice mixture and set aside.

In a saucepot, sauté spinach, add heavy cream, and reduce.

Sear the steak on each side for 4 minutes.

Serve on a plate and garnish with parsley.

SHRIMP SKEWERS

10 each shrimp, peeled and deveined

0.5 ounces oregano, finely chopped

0.5 ounces rosemary, finely chopped

0.5 ounces thyme, finely chopped

1.5 ounces olive oil

kosher salt and black pepper to taste

2 each wooden skewers

0.5 ounces cilantro, chopped

0.5 each lime, juiced

Soak the skewers in water.

Toss shrimp in herbs, olive oil, salt, and pepper.

Place 5 shrimp on each skewer.

Grill each side for 2 minutes or until shrimp turns pink.

Place skewers on a plate, squeeze lime juice over them, and sprinkle with cilantro.

PASTA WITH SHRIMP AND OLIVES

0.5 ounce rosemary, chopped

0.5 ounce thyme, chopped

0.5 ounce crushed red pepper flakes

2 ounce Kalamata olives, sliced

5.5 ounce shrimp, peeled and deveined

7.5 ounce angel hair pasta, boiled

kosher salt and black pepper to taste

3 each basil leaves, chiffonade, fried

Boil pasta in salted water.

In a sauté pan, combine shrimp, olives, and herbs.

Cook until shrimp turns pink.

Toss in the angel hair pasta.

Serve each plate with pasta at the center and garnish with fried basil leaves.

FILLET OF SOLE WITH EGGPLANT

3 lbs Dover sole

2 lbs eggplant, cubed and soaked in lemon juice

2 ounces dill, minced

2 ounces tarragon, minced

2 ounces fennel seeds, toasted and ground

2 ounces kosher salt

1 ounce black pepper

½ ounce fresh grated nutmeg

4 ounces extra virgin olive oil

Mix together herbs and seasonings, then divide into equal parts.

Season the sole fillets with the herb mixture and set aside.

Drain the lemon juice from the eggplant, pat dry, season with the remaining herb mixture, toss in olive oil, and place on a roasting pan. Roast at 425 degrees for 10-15 minutes.

Sauté the sole in the remaining olive oil, presentation side down first, 2-3 minutes per side.

BRAISED RABBIT WITH BUTTERED NOODLES

3 pounds rabbit, sectioned

4 carrots, peeled and quartered

10 celery stalks, large diced

5 garlic cloves, peeled and smashed

10 onions, peeled and quartered

5 fennel, peeled and quartered

1 ½ lbs egg noodles or tagliatelle

3 sprigs thyme

2 sprigs rosemary

2 sprigs tarragon

2 ounces flour

7 ounces tomato paste

1 bottle red wine

10 ounces water

Kosher salt and black pepper

2 ounces olive oil

Preheat the oven to 350 degrees.

Heat a Dutch oven on the stove, add oil, vegetables, aromatics, and tomato paste.

Coat the rabbit in flour, shaking off excess. Sear in pan and then add to the vegetables and aromatics.

Deglaze with red wine, season with salt and pepper.

Add half of the water, cover with a lid, and braise in the oven for 30 minutes.

Boil the pasta.

Serving Suggestion: Arrange the pasta at the bottom of a platter, then top with the braised vegetables. Lastly, place the braised rabbit pieces on top and garnish with chopped fennel fronds.

STUFFED SQUID WITH TOMATO SAUCE

4 pounds squid, cleaned

18 ounces fresh tomato sauce

1 bottle red wine

2 ounces basil, minced

2 ounces Italian parsley, minced

2 ounces rosemary, minced

2 ounces kosher salt

1 ounce black pepper

3 ounces olive oil

1 ½ ounces unsalted butter

1 recipe risotto, prepared and cooled

Season the squids and carefully stuff each with the cooled risotto using a spoon.

Pour the wine into a sauce pot and simmer for 5 minutes.

Add the tomato sauce and cook together for an additional 10-15 minutes.

In a sauté pan, sauté the squid in batches to avoid overcrowding.

Cook each batch for about 1 minute.

Simmer the sautéed squid in the tomato sauce for about 5 minutes or until tender.

RICOTTA GNOCCHI

½ cup all-purpose flour, sifted 3 times

2 teaspoons salt

½ egg, beaten

1 pound ricotta, drained overnight in cheesecloth

1 teaspoon sugar (omit for savory gnocchi)

¼ teaspoon fresh grated nutmeg

salt and pepper (if making savory gnocchi)

In a bowl, combine ricotta, egg, and salt.

Once combined, gently incorporate flour.

Transfer the mixture to a piping bag fitted with a three-quarter inch tip.

Pipe into 1-inch pieces and place in flour. Roll each piece into balls.

Boil in salted water for 3-4 minutes or until they float.

Remove with a slotted spoon and set on a platter.

For savory gnocchi: Serve with browned butter and sage or a light tomato sauce. Garnish with shaved parmesan and toasted pine nuts.

For sweet gnocchi: Serve with a raspberry sauce or a curd and garnish with diced apples or toasted nuts.

POMMES CHATEAU

2 pounds
russet potatoes, tourneed

kosher salt and black pepper to taste

½ pound
unsalted butter

½ cup
chopped parsley

Peel and wash potatoes and immerse them in cold water.

Tournee the potatoes into seven-sided, football shapes, each about 1.5 inches long.

Parboil the potatoes for 4-6 minutes. Drain, let them cool, and dry before cooking further.
Sauté potatoes in butter until they turn tender and achieve a golden brown hue.

Season with salt, pepper, and parsley.

WARM SCALLOP SALAD WITH TOMATO, MINT, AND LIME VINAIGRETTE

Dressing:

5 ounces extra virgin olive oil

1 ½ tablespoons shallot, minced

1 ½ tablespoons fresh lime juice

½ teaspoon kosher salt

½ teaspoon black pepper

1 ½ cups tomatoes, peeled, seeded, and diced

Salad:

12 ounces scallops, well-drained and patted dry
2 tablespoons olive oil

2 ounces jicama, peeled and julienne

1 bunch watercress, larger items removed

1 bunch arugula

Heat olive oil and sauté shallots until they turn soft. Avoid browning the shallots.

Remove from heat, then add lime juice, salt, pepper, and tomatoes.

If using sea scallops, remove the white muscle.

Heat olive oil, add scallops, and sauté over medium-high heat until just cooked with a slight translucence in the middle. Remove from heat.

Pour half of the dressing over the warm scallops in the pan. Adjust seasoning and keep warm.

Evenly distribute greens among plates.Place scallops dressed in the center of the greens.

Sprinkle jicama over the salad and spoon on additional dressing as desired.

THE SWEET YEARS

As our culinary journey draws to a close, I find myself reminiscing about this section, which was particularly challenging. As a dedicated pastry chef, I aimed to curate a collection of desserts that ranged from simple delights to more sophisticated creations. Some of these treats have been my personal favorites for years, while others are newer additions that have quickly earned their place. It's my sincere hope that these desserts resonate with you as they have with me. Remember, life always feels a bit brighter with something sweet on the plate. Here's to indulgence and joy!

CLASSIC FUDGE

1 cup semisweet chocolate morsels

1 cup butterscotch morsels

14 ounces sweetened condensed milk

1 teaspoon pure vanilla extract

1 cup nuts (optional)

Combine chocolate, butterscotch, vanilla, and nuts in a large mixing bowl. Set aside.

In a saucepan, heat condensed milk over medium until it slightly boils.

Pour the heated milk over the chocolate mixture and stir until fully melted.

Transfer the mixture into a buttered 13x9-inch baking dish. Chill for 2-4 hours. Slice into squares to serve.

Variations: Elevate this fudge by incorporating dried fruits like cherries, blueberries, or mango. For a nutty twist, swirl in some peanut butter.

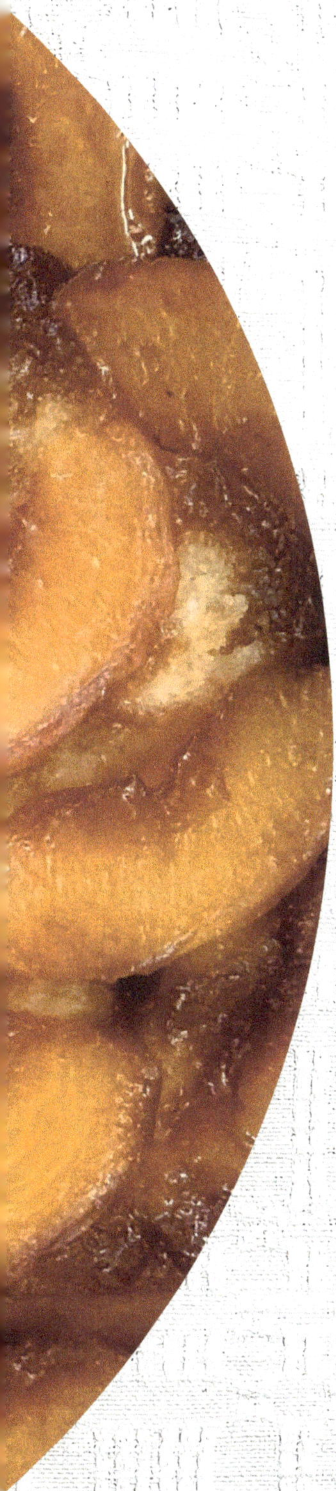

PEACH UPSIDE DOWN CAKE

1 pound peaches

2 ounces toasted slivered almonds

8 ounces softened unsalted butter

4 ounces brown sugar

4 ounces granulated sugar

2 eggs

1 teaspoon pure vanilla extract

6 ounces all-purpose flour

½ tablespoon baking powder

2 ounces heavy cream

2 ounces freshly squeezed orange juice

Preheat oven to 350 degrees.

Slice peaches into wedges.

Melt 2 ounces of butter in a 9-inch round cake pan, ensuring both bottom and sides are coated. Sprinkle with brown sugar.

Place half the almonds and arrange peach slices decoratively over them.

Top with remaining sugar and almonds.

In a bowl, cream the rest of the butter with sugar. Add eggs one at a time, then vanilla. Sift flour with baking powder and salt. Combine cream and orange juice, and alternate adding these with the flour mixture to your butter mix.

Carefully spoon batter over peaches and bake for 35-40 minutes.

Let cool for 10 minutes before inverting.

Serving Suggestion: Best enjoyed slightly warm with whipped or clotted cream.

KIWI CRÉME PIE

Crust:

4 ounces
all-purpose flour

2 ounces
granulated sugar

1 teaspoon
lemon zest

4 ounces
unsalted butter, diced

1 egg yolk

Filling:

8 ounces
cream cheese

8 ounces
sour cream

2 eggs

2 ounces
granulated sugar

½ teaspoon
pure vanilla extract

½ teaspoon
lemon zest

Topping:

8 ounces
cream cheese

1 ounce
granulated sugar

½ ounce
lemon juice

3 kiwis, sliced

For crust:
Blend flour, sugar, zest, butter, and egg yolk until a dough forms.

Chill for 30 minutes.

Preheat oven to 400 degrees, roll dough, and line pie pan.

Parbake for 10 minutes, then cool.

For filling:
Combine ingredients and pour into crust. Bake at a reduced temperature of 350 degrees for 30 minutes.

For topping:
Whisk together cream cheese, sugar, and lemon juice. Spread over the pie.

Chill before garnishing with kiwi.

BROWNIE PUDDING CAKE

1 cup all-purpose flour

¾ cup cocoa powder, unsweetened

1 teaspoon baking powder

½ teaspoon salt

1 cup granulated sugar

3 ounces unsalted butter, melted

4 ounces heavy cream

2 eggs

1 teaspoon vanilla

10 ounces water

¼ cup light brown sugar

Preheat oven to 350 degrees.

Sift together the dry ingredients.

In a mixer, blend sugar, butter, cream, eggs, and vanilla.

Incorporate the dry mixture. Spread in an 8-inch square baking pan.

Combine cocoa, boiling water, and brown sugar.

Pour over batter.

Bake for around 35 minutes.

Serving Suggestion: Pair with whipped cream or vanilla ice cream. To impress, serve in ramekins with a hint of espresso and orange zest.

MEXICAN WEDDING COOKIES

1 cup unsalted butter, softened

½ cup powdered sugar, sifted

1 tablespoon vanilla

2 ¼ cup flour, sifted

½ tablespoon salt

¾ cup pecans, finely chopped

powdered sugar as needed to roll cookies

Preheat oven to 400 degrees.

Mix butter, powdered sugar, and vanilla.

Sift flour and salt, then combine.

Stir in pecans.

APPLE FRITTERS

2 ½ cups all-purpose flour, plus ½ cup for dredging

1 cup cornmeal

½ cup brown sugar

2 tablespoons baking soda

1 teaspoon salt

2 cups buttermilk

1 ½ cups water

2 eggs

2 teaspoons vanilla extract

3 Granny Smith apples, cored and cut into ¼-inch rings

In a medium bowl, mix together the dry ingredients.

In a separate bowl, whisk together the wet ingredients.

Gradually add the wet ingredients to the dry, mixing until a batter forms.

Dredge apple rings in the extra flour, then coat in batter.

Fry until golden brown, approximately 2 minutes per side.

LEMON BLISS GRANITA

1 cup water

¾ cup + 1 tablespoon sugar

2/3 cup fresh lemon juice, strained

¾ cup whole milk ricotta, drained

pinch of salt

1 tablespoon lemon zest

crushed amaretti cookies (for garnish)

In a medium saucepan, stir water and ¾ cup of sugar over high heat until sugar dissolves.

Transfer to a freezer-safe container, and freeze. Stir occasionally until the liquid is slushy, about 2 hours.

Use a fork to scrape every 30 minutes until fully crystallized.

In a separate bowl, whisk together ricotta, the remaining sugar, salt, and lemon zest.

Serve granita in martini glasses, dollop with ricotta mixture, and garnish with crushed amaretti cookies.

ASIAN PEARS AND MACADAMIA WONTONS

1 Asian pear, seeded and diced to ¼ inch

4 macadamia nuts, finely chopped

4 ounces coconut milk

1 tablespoon fresh lemon juice

12 wonton wrappers, cut into circles

powdered sugar (for dusting)

honey (for serving)

Combine pear, nuts, coconut milk, and lemon juice in a saucepan.

Simmer until mixture is almost dry, about 20 minutes.

Allow to cool.

Place a spoonful of filling on one wonton circle, moisten edges with water, then top with another wonton circle. Press edges to seal. Repeat with remaining wontons.

Freeze the filled wo ntons briefly until firm.

Fry in 375-degree oil until browned. Drain on paper towels.

Dust with powdered sugar and serve with honey.

KEY LIME PIE

Crust:

5 ounces graham cracker crumbs

2 ounces sugar

2 ounces melted butter

Filling:

15 ounces sweetened condensed milk

6 egg yolks

6 ounces key lime juice

1 tablespoon lime zest

Topping:

8 ounces heavy cream

2 ounces powdered sugar

For the crust:
Combine graham cracker crumbs and sugar in a bowl. Mix in melted butter until combined. Press into a 9″ pie pan.

For the filling:
Whisk together sweetened condensed milk, egg yolks, lime juice, and lime zest. Pour into the prepared crust.

Bake in a preheated oven at 350 degrees for approximately 15 minutes or until set. Let the pie cool at room temperature for 1 hour.

For the topping:
Whip heavy cream with powdered sugar until soft peaks form, avoiding over-whipping. Spread or pipe over cooled pie.

CRANBERRY MARMALADE

2 ounces water

2 ounces granulated sugar

2 ounces brown sugar

1 ounce orange juice

12 ounces cranberries, fresh or frozen

1 pinch of cinnamon

1 teaspoon orange zest

2 ounces orange segments

1 ounce dried lavender (optional)

Combine sugars, orange juice, and water in a saucepan; bring to a boil.

Add cranberries and cinnamon; simmer until cranberries burst (about 15 minutes).

Stir in orange zest and continue simmering until desired consistency is reached.

If using, fold in dried lavender.

COCONUT BALLS

1 pound
sweetened flaked coconut

¾ cup
toasted walnuts, chopped

¼ cup
macadamia nuts, chopped

2 cups
powdered sugar

2 tablespoons
white corn syrup

1 teaspoon cognac

In a large bowl, combine all ingredients until well mixed.

Using a small ice cream scoop or your hands, form into balls.

Refrigerate until firm and ready to serve.

PEAR HONEY

1 20-ounce can crushed pineapple with syrup

6 pounds pears, peeled, cored, and chopped

10 cups granulated sugar

1 tablespoon fresh lemon juice

1 cinnamon stick

3 whole cloves

½ cup water

Combine all ingredients in a saucepan. Cook over medium heat.

Simmer until pears are tender and mixture has thickened, about 15-20 minutes depending on pear ripeness.

FLORAL BREAD CAKE

1 pound soft dinner rolls, chopped

2 egg whites

2 whole eggs

1 ½ cups granulated sugar

2 ½ cups milk

¼ teaspoon vanilla extract

1 teaspoon orange blossom water

½ cup toasted walnuts

Preheat oven to 350 degrees.

Grease a bundt pan.

In a large bowl, whisk together eggs, egg whites, sugar, milk, vanilla, and orange blossom water.

Fold in the chopped bread, ensuring it's well soaked, about 15-20 minutes.

Pour mixture into the prepared bundt pan and bake for about 1 hour or until set.

Let the cake rest for 10 minutes before inverting onto a plate.

ZUCCHINI BREAD

3 ¼ cups all-purpose flour

1 ½ teaspoons salt

1 teaspoon nutmeg

2 teaspoons baking soda

1 teaspoon cinnamon

3 cups sugar

1 cup vegetable oil

4 eggs, beaten

⅓ cup water

1 cup pecans, chopped

Preheat oven to 350 degrees.

In a large bowl, combine flour, salt, nutmeg, baking soda, cinnamon, and sugar.

Mix wet ingredients into dry ingredients. Fold in nuts.

Bake for 1 hour or until a tester comes out clean.

LEMON CRUMB BAR COOKIES

Crust:

8 ounces unsalted butter, softened

10 ounces granulated sugar

2 eggs

18 ounces cake flour

For the Crust: Cream butter, sugar, and eggs in a mixer for 3 minutes on speed 2. Add flour and mix until blended. Spread in a buttered half sheet pan. Parbake at 350 degrees for 15 minutes.

Filling:

24 ounces granulated sugar

2 ounces cornstarch

6 eggs

6 ounces fresh lemon juice

1 lemon, zested

For the Filling: Whisk sugar and cornstarch. Add eggs, lemon juice, and zest. Mix until combined. Pour over parbaked crust. Bake at 350 degrees for 10 minutes.

Topping:

8 ounces all-purpose flour

6 ounces granulated sugar

4 ounces unsalted butter

For the Topping: In a food processor, combine flour, sugar, and butter until pea-sized crumbles form. Sprinkle over filling. Bake at 350 degrees for 15-20 minutes. Cool, then cut into 20 squares.

SAUTERNE ZABAGLIONE WITH ROASTED GRAPES

4 large egg yolks

¼ cup granulated sugar

¼ cup sauterne or dry marsala

roasted grapes (see below for recipe)

Bring pot of water to a simmer over low heat.

Combine egg yolks and sugar in a heat-resistant bowl. Whisk until foamy.

Place bowl over simmering water (ensure bottom doesn't touch the water). Whisk constantly.

Gradually add sauterne, continuing to whisk. Do not boil. Whisk vigorously for about 5 minutes or until custard doubles in volume.

Spoon into dessert bowls. Serve with roasted grapes.

ROASTED GRAPES:

¼ pound white seedless grapes

¼ pound red seedless grapes

½ pound purple seedless grapes

Preheat oven to 400 degrees

Halve grapes and place on a sheet tray.

Roast for 10-15 minutes or until grapes begin to wrinkle. Let cool.

CHOCOLATE PLUM STRUDEL

1 recipe
flaky pie dough

3-4 ripe plums, diced

3 tablespoons chocolate hazelnut spread

4 ounces nuts (optional)

Roll the pie dough into a medium rectangle shape.

Cut 1 ½ -inch strips on each side, leaving room in the center for the filling.

Spread the chocolate hazelnut spread on the pastry center, then layer with plums and nuts.

Braid the pastry strips overlapping each other. Place on a sheet pan, brush with an egg wash, and sprinkle with sugar.

Bake at 350 degrees until golden brown.

Tip: Egg wash =
1 egg yolk mixed with
1 tablespoon water.

Serving Suggestion:
Serve with fresh whipped cream.

FRUIT SALAD WITH HONEY-YOGURT SAUCE

1 cup vanilla low-fat yogurt

1 tablespoon honey

1 ⅓ teaspoon grated lime rind

3 cups cubed pineapple

1 ½ cups chopped Braeburn apple

1 cup chopped peeled kiwi

⅓ cup sweetened flaked coconut

1 medium banana, sliced

¼ cup toasted slivered almonds

Mix yogurt, honey, and lime rind in a small bowl.

In a large bowl, combine pineapple, apple, kiwi, and coconut. Toss gently.

Just before serving, add banana slices.

Top with yogurt sauce and sprinkle with almonds.

Tips: Prepare and refrigerate the yogurt sauce up to a day in advance. Fruit mixture (excluding banana) can be refrigerated up to 3 hours ahead.

MANGO BREAD

1 cup all-purpose flour

1 teaspoon baking soda

½ teaspoon cinnamon

¼ teaspoon salt

¾ cup granulated sugar

1 cup diced ripe mango

2 eggs, beaten

6 tablespoon vegetable oil

½ teaspoon vanilla extract

½ cup chopped macadamia nuts

Preheat oven to 350 degrees.

Sift together flour, baking soda, cinnamon, and salt. Set aside.

In another bowl, combine sugar, mango, eggs, oil, and vanilla.

Mix the dry ingredients with the wet. Blend for a minute. Add macadamia nuts and mix.

Pour into a greased and floured loaf pan.

Bake for 40-45 minutes or until a toothpick is clean.

LEMON PUDDING CAKES

1 recipe lemon curd, cooled

2 tablespoon all-purpose flour, sifted

½ cup milk

3 egg whites

1 pinch cream of tartar

5 tablespoons sugar

Mix lemon curd, flour, and milk. Set aside.

Whip egg whites until foamy. Add cream of tartar and whip to soft peaks.

Add sugar and whip to stiff peaks.

Carefully fold egg whites into lemon curd mixture in thirds.

Fill ramekins and bake at 325 degrees for 20-30 minutes.

LEMON CURD

2/3 cup
granulated sugar

2 tablespoons
lemon zest

3 large eggs

4 large egg yolks

½ cup fresh squeezed
lemon juice

¼ cup fresh squeezed
lime juice

4 tablespoons (½ stick)
unsalted butter,
cut into ½ inch cubes
and chilled

Prepare an ice bath by filling a large bowl with ice.

Fill a medium saucepan ¾ full of water and bring it to a simmer over medium heat.

In a food processor, combine sugar and lemon zest. Pulse until the sugar turns yellow and gives off a fragrant aroma.

Alternatively, you can achieve this using a mortar and pestle.

In a separate bowl, whisk together the lemon-infused sugar, eggs, and egg yolks for about 30 seconds to ensure even distribution of the sugar. This step helps in preventing the eggs from coagulating prematurely.

Place this bowl over the simmering water, ensuring it doesn't touch the water.

Continuously whisk until the sugar has dissolved. If the mixture feels grainy, keep whisking.

Incorporate the lemon and lime juices. Continue whisking constantly for about 5 minutes. Use a rubber spatula occasionally to scrape the sides and bottom of the bowl, ensuring even cooking.

Check the temperature of the curd; it should reach 160 degrees and have the consistency of sour cream.

Once done, remove the bowl from heat. Transfer the mixture to a separate bowl and whisk in the chilled butter until the mixture is smooth.

Strain the curd through a cheesecloth into a clean bowl to remove any lumps.

To prevent a skin from forming on top, place plastic wrap directly onto the surface of the curd. Let it cool.

Tip: Ensure the plastic wrap is in direct contact with the curd to prevent skin formation.

Substitutions:
This curd can be adapted using various citrus fruits such as orange, grapefruit, passion fruit, etc.

Serving Suggestions:
This versatile dessert sauce can be paired with an array of items. Enjoy it with scones, cookies, or ice cream.

FOCACCIA

1 pound and 9 ounces unbleached bread flour, sifted

2 ½ cups water

2 tablespoon + 1 teaspoon granulated sugar

2 tablespoon kosher salt

1 packet instant yeast

10 tablespoon extra virgin olive oil

2 teaspoon rosemary, minced

In a large bowl, combine all ingredients. Use a wooden spoon to mix until partially combined.

Ditch the spoon and mix with clean hands until smooth (dough will be slightly sticky).

Cover with a tea towel or plastic wrap and let rise in a warm place for about 2 hours or until doubled in size.

Preheat the oven to 475 degrees.

Oil a sheet pan with olive oil.

Transfer the risen dough to the sheet pan and spread it out evenly.

Allow to rise again, covered with a tea towel.

Once risen, create dimples in the dough with your fingertips.

Sprinkle with sea salt.

Place the pan in the oven and immediately reduce heat to 450 degrees. Bake for 15 minutes, rotate the pan, and continue baking until golden brown.

Tip: Customize your focaccia by trying different herbs like oregano or thyme. Or go sweet with ingredients like raisins, anise, or vanilla.

SUGAR COOKIES

6 ounces unsalted butter, cold and cut into pieces

½ cup granulated sugar

¼ teaspoon salt

1 teaspoon vanilla bean paste or vanilla extract

1 ¾ cup all-purpose flour, sifted

1 egg

Cream butter until pale yellow.

Add sugar, salt, and vanilla. Cream until light and fluffy.

Add the egg and mix until just incorporated.

Gently fold in the sifted flour.

Wrap the dough in plastic wrap and chill for 1 hour.

Preheat oven to 350 degrees.

Roll out the cookie dough and cut using a cookie cutter.

Place on a baking sheet and bake until golden brown.

APPLE FRANGIPANE TART

For the dough:

2 sticks unsalted butter, cubed

¼ cup granulated sugar

4 cups all-purpose flour

3 egg yolks

3 tablespoons water

3 tablespoons heavy cream

For the frangipane:

¼ cup unsalted butter

½ cup powdered sugar

¾ cup almond meal flour

1 tablespoon unbleached flour

1 large egg

1 teaspoon vanilla

For the apples:

4 medium Granny Smith apples, peeled, cored, and sliced

¼ cup granulated sugar

½ teaspoon cinnamon

⅛ teaspoon allspice

4 teaspoon butter

For the dough: In a food processor, pulse together butter, sugar, and flour until the mixture looks like small pearls. Slowly add in water and heavy cream, pulsing until a dough forms. Form into a disc, wrap in plastic, and refrigerate overnight.

For the frangipane: In a large bowl, cream butter and powdered sugar until fluffy. Beat in the almond meal and white flour. Add the egg and vanilla and mix until combined.

For the apples: In a bowl, combine apples, sugar, cinnamon, and allspice.

To assemble: Roll out the chilled dough on a floured surface to about ¼-inch thickness. Fit into a tart shell and place in the freezer for 5 minutes.

Remove and spread frangipane evenly over the dough. Arrange apple slices on top in a circular pattern. Brush with melted butter and sprinkle with the sugar mixture.

Bake in a preheated 375-degree oven for 18-20 minutes or until golden brown.

OLD TOWN
THE
BEST
YEARS

The time has come not to say goodbye, but to leave the rest up to you. These are the best years, a time when the path ahead is yours to choose. It's only fitting that the final chapter in my story revolves around delightful libations. Whether you prefer a spirited kick or a refreshing non-alcoholic option, these drinks are bound to satisfy every thirst.

CLASSIC EGG CREAMS

2 ½ ounces whole milk

8 ounces seltzer water

1 ounces chocolate syrup

Chill the milk in the freezer.

Drizzle chocolate syrup into a glass, then pour in the chilled milk.

Slowly add the seltzer while vigorously stirring with a long-handled spoon.

Serving Suggestion:
Serve in a tall glass, such as a malt glass or a highball.

SUMMER-GIRL SODA

¾ cup fresh or frozen raspberries

½ teaspoon sugar

1 ¼ cups vanilla ice cream, divided

1 ½ cups chilled club soda, divided

Press raspberries through a sieve or fine colander over a bowl to remove seeds.

Mix raspberry pulp with sugar.

Divide raspberry mixture among 4 parfait glasses.

Add ¼ of ice cream to each glass and stir. Pour ½ cup of club soda into each glass.

Garnish with fresh raspberries.

SPARKLING FRUIT PUNCH

1 can (6 ounce) frozen lemonade

1 can (6 ounce) frozen orange juice

1 can (6 ounce) frozen pineapple juice

2 cans (46 ounce) fruit punch

2 quarts water

2 quarts ginger ale

1 quart soda

Mix the first five ingredients, then add 1 quart of ginger ale and 1 quart of soda.

Just before serving, add the remaining ginger ale.

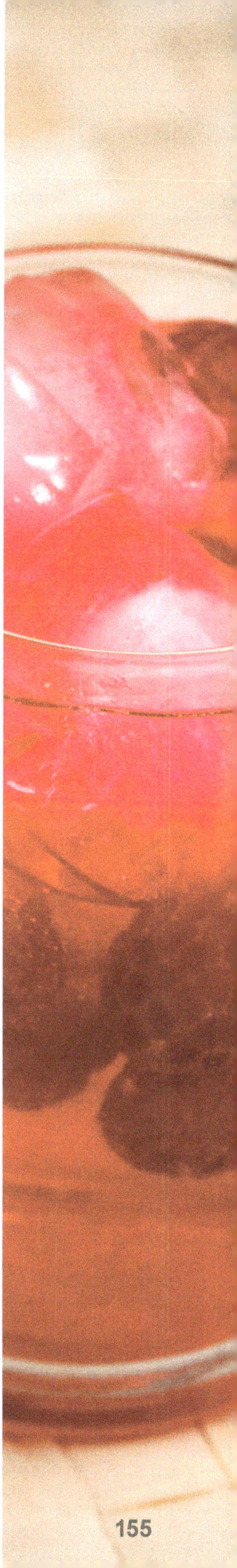

STRAWBERRY SPARKLER

1 package (10 ounce) frozen strawberries, thawed

2 cups chilled cranberry juice

1 bottle (750 milliliters) prosecco, chilled (Champagne can be substituted)

Blend strawberries until smooth.

Pour into a pitcher and stir in cranberry juice and prosecco.

Serve immediately.

REFRESHING SPARKLER

1 package (10 ounce) frozen strawberries, thawed

Blend strawberries until smooth and pour into a serving pitcher.

2 cups chilled cranberry juice

Stir in cranberry juice and sparkling grape juice.

1 liter bottle sparkling grape juice, chilled

Serve immediately.

CHERRIES JUBILEE MARTINI

3 ounces marshmallow vodka

1 ounces maraschino cherry juice

Splash of lemon juice

Shake well in a chilled cocktail shaker.

Drizzle the inside of a martini glass with chocolate syrup.

Pour the mixture into the glass and serve.

MANGO MOJITO SPRITZER

¼ cup golden rum

¼ cup mango puree

3 sprigs of mint

**¼ - ½ cup
Perrier bottled water**

Chill the glass in the freezer until ready to serve.

Muddle ice with mint in the glass, then mix in rum, mango puree, and water.

Pour into the chilled glass and garnish with a slice of mango and a sprig of mint.

For a margarita version, blend the ingredients in a mixer.

BLOOD ORANGE DIVINITY

¼ cup
blood orange juice

¼ bottle of Prosecco

splash of heavy cream

Stir the ingredients in a pitcher and pour into a chilled tall glass.

APPLE PIE IN THE SKY

1 cup hard apple cider

¼ cup apple liqueur

½ cup club soda

Shake well in a chilled cocktail shaker, then pour into a martini glass.

Optionally, top with alcohol-flavored whipped cream or regular whipped cream.

SANGRIA

1 bottle Lillet

¼ cup raspberry nectar

¼ cup guava nectar

¼ cup lychee nectar

1 can of coconut water

Mix the ingredients in a pitcher and enjoy the delightful concoction.

May these recipes bring
a flavorful and refreshing twist
to your culinary adventures.

**Cheers to
your journey ahead!**

Bibliography

Paterson, John.
Choosing your Wine: A Regional Guide to the Best of the World's Wines.
London: The Hamlyn Publishing Group Limited, 1980.

Ozias, Blake.
All about Wine.
New York: Blake Ozias, 1966.

Yard, Sherry.
The Secrets of Baking: Simple Techniques for Sophisticated Desserts.
New York: Houghton Mifflin Company, 2003.

Labensky, Sarah R., and Hause, Alan M.
On Cooking: A Textbook of Culinary Fundamentals,
Third Edition. Upper Saddle River, New Jersey: Pearson Custom Publishing, 2005.

www.ingramcontent.com/pod-product-compliance
Ingram Content Group UK Ltd.
Pitfield, Milton Keynes, MK11 3LW, UK
UKHW060125010826
14089UKWH00006B/157